shibori knitted felt

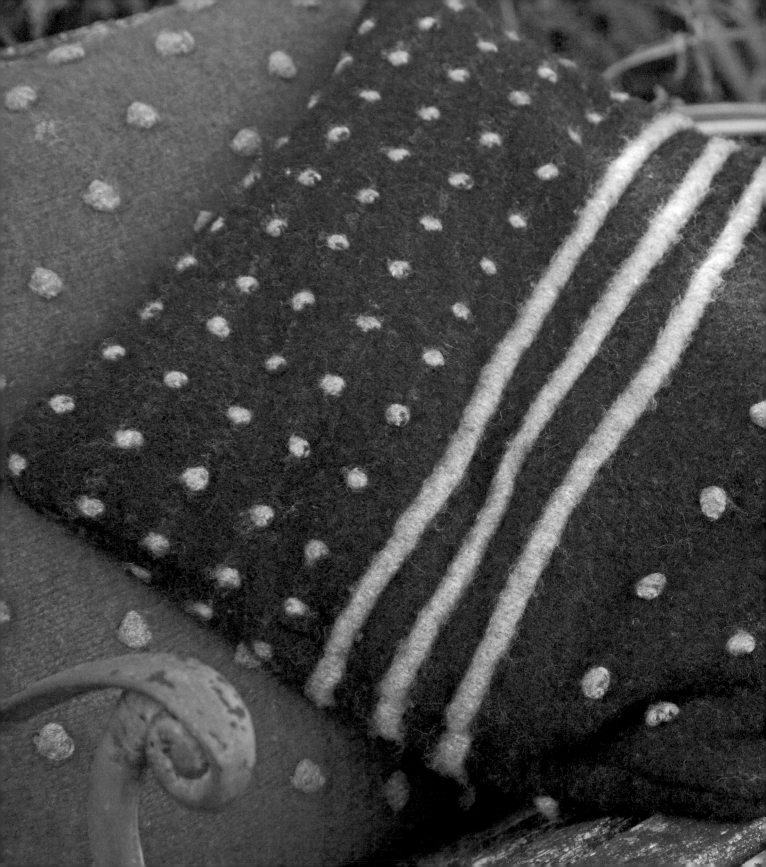

shibori
knitted
felt

ALISON CROWTHER-SMITH

PHOTOGRAPHS BY JOHN HESELTINE

INTERWEAVE PRESS.
interweavebooks.com

This book is dedicated to Emma Mary Knowles, who started it all.

SHIBORI KNITTED FELT

 INTERWEAVE PRESS.
Interweavebooks.com

First published in 2008 in North America by
Interweave Press, LLC
201 East Fourth Street
Loveland, CO 80537
interweavebooks.com

Editor Sally Harding
Designer Anne Wilson
Stylist Susan Berry
Pattern writer Sue Whiting
Pattern checker Jean Marshall
Illustrations Carrie Hill

Associate Publisher Susan Berry

Library of Congress Cataloging-in-Publication Data
Crowther-Smith, Alison.
  Shibori knitted felt : 20 plus designs to knit, bead, and felt / Alison
    Crowther-Smith, author.
      p. cm.
  Includes index.
  ISBN-13: 978-1-59668-085-2 (pbk.)
  1. Felt work. 2. Felting. 3. Tie-dyeing. 4. Beadwork. I. Title.
  TT849.5.C76 2008
  746'.0463--dc22
                        2007040046

10 9 8 7 6 5 4 3 2 1

Reproduced and printed in China

contents

introduction

Felted hand knits can be beautiful and delicate in appearance and at the same time have the practical qualities of strong and durable felted wool fabric. This book is about creating unique and attractive items for you and for your home—everyday objects that are at the same time lovely to look at and to use. It is also about the magical transformation that your knitting goes through in order to become felt. By combining your practical knitting skills with the alchemy of felting in your washing machine you can literally transform your knitting, adding an entirely new dimension to it.

The fresh twist to the designs in this book comes from the application of traditional Shibori fabric techniques or Shibori-inspired textures to the projects. Applying Shibori to hand-knitted felt is a unique way to introduce extra elements of texture, shape, and creativity. The results are not the clumpy, bulky felts that one so often thinks of in relation to hand-knitted felts. Instead they exemplify the stylish, simple, softly yielding fabrics that you can make with these easy techniques—combining practicality with artistry.

I hope this book conveys to you my passion for this craft. The projects, many of them simple and straightforward, are designed to get you started with Shibori felting and to tempt you to go further.

I have included a comprehensive section on how to felt your knitting and how to apply the main easy-to-learn Shibori techniques (see pages 104–109). This section also explains how to achieve the right size for your finished felted pieces, so you can go on to adapt any of my designs or produce your very own knitted felt creations.

The felting process

It is important to understand what is happening to your knitting once you put it in the washing machine, especially when you start to apply Shibori techniques to it.

The essential elements for felting your wool knitting are: hot water, laundry detergent, and agitation or friction. These components actually change the structure of the wool yarn. The wool fibers swell up in the hot water, then the friction of the machine action makes their swollen scales rub against each other and catch so that they become matted together. The scales of the wool are locked into place, causing the fabric to thicken while shrinking in width and especially in length. Wool also contains keratin, which swells into a jelly-like substance when heated, further aiding the felting process.

When you create a piece of knitting, you have effectively woven a piece of fabric with your yarn and needles. Felting it reduces the size of the fabric, but not its overall volume: felting takes nothing away, it simply rearranges it, hence the thicker feel to the fabric.

Shibori felting

Shibori is a term used to describe the process of introducing resistant elements into textiles. It is an ancient Japanese craft, usually thought of in the context of dyes applied to fabric. The word shibori comes from the Japanese word *shiboru*—meaning to wring out, squeeze, or press. At its simplest level, tie-dyeing is Shibori, where the tied or twisted fabric is immersed in dye, but the dye can only penetrate into part of the fabric, leaving the tie-dye patterns that we may know and love from the 1970s.

Shibori can be a highly complex craft, and there are many different types of Shibori. It is, at one level, a real art form because amazing pieces of Shibori fabric art have been produced. Applied to fabric, Shibori is used to create three-dimensional textures and colors by using heat, pleating, and dyeing.

On a more practical level, the basic principles of Shibori can be applied to knitted wool fabric. The techniques for this are easy and effective. To practice these techniques, you need to remember that the fabric you have knitted will shrink everywhere—unless you prevent it from doing so. To prevent the shrinkage, you need to introduce a "resist." For example, where a marble is tied into the knitting to create a "bump," the fabric stretched around that marble cannot move and therefore it cannot felt like the rest of the knitting. Once the resisting item—the marble—is removed, the fabric that was around it is still intact and you can see the original knitted stitches on these "bumps" (see page 50).

Similarly, when pleats are sewn into the knitting prior to felting, the areas within the pleats cannot agitate and felt, so once the work is dry and the stitches are removed, the unfelted areas are revealed. In this case, the sewing of the pleats provides the "resist" (see pages 28 and 29).

I have experimented with many different resisting objects—tying marbles, pebbles, and coins into samples of knitting—to see what the finished felted material looks like. I have also tried out Shibori-inspired textures on felted knitting, for example, knitted-in or sewn-on beads, felted embroidery, and knitted-in bobbles and three-dimensional ridges. Some results are better than others, but all are fascinating.

For uniformity and predictability, I have used marbles, wooden beads, and hand-pleating as the main traditional Shibori applications in the book—but you should try out whatever you think might be interesting! This book covers all the techniques you need to take your felting skills forward in your own unique way.

Alison Crowther-Smith

projects

sheer scarf and wrap

Very delicate and beautifully simple, this sheer scarf and wrap are knitted in Rowan *Scottish Tweed 4-Ply* and *Kidsilk Haze*. The silk in the *Kidsilk Haze* provides a resist to the felting process and the *Scottish Tweed* felts gently, so the felted effect is subdued. The resulting fabric is sheer and subtly striped. As a rule, you can't felt with *Kidsilk Haze* unless you provide a structure, such as the stripes of alternating yarns that I have used for this scarf. And you certainly can't felt it on its own, unless you want felted pebbles.

The scarf can be worked plain or beaded, and in a choice of three colorways. It is felted *before* the ruffle at each end is added, and there are two ruffles to choose from. To emphasize the simple drama of the beaded wrap, I didn't add a ruffle, but you could easily knit one on if you like.

sheer scarf

Finished size
Completed scarf measures approximately 6¼" (16cm) wide by 62¼" (158cm) long, excluding ruffle.

Yarn
2 x ⅞oz (25g) balls of Rowan *Kidsilk Haze* in **A** (Violetta 633, Jelly 597, or Nightly 585)
3 x ⅞oz (25g) balls of Rowan *Scottish Tweed 4-Ply* in **B** (Thistle 016, Apple 015, or Midnight 023)

Needles
Pair of size 3 (3.25mm) knitting needles

Notions
Beaded scarf only: Approximately 550 crystal 4mm glass beads

Gauge before felting
26 sts and 38 rows to 4" (10cm) measured over stockinette stitch using B and size 3 (3.25mm) needles *or size necessary to obtain correct gauge.*

Abbreviations
bead 1 = bring yarn to front (RS) of work between two needles, slide bead up next to st just worked, slip next stitch purlwise from left needle to right needle and take yarn back (WS) of work between two needles leaving bead sitting on RS of work in front of slipped st.
See also page 109.

Special note
You can carry the *Kidsilk Haze* yarn up the side of the work from stripe to stripe, loosely twisting the two yarns together at the end of the row—this reduces the number of ends to darn in. But do not carry the *Scottish Tweed 4-Ply* from stripe to stripe because it will shrink when felted.

Scarf without beads
Work exactly as given for Beaded Scarf (below), but omitting beads by replacing each "bead 1" with "K1."

Beaded scarf
Thread beads onto B (see page 17).
Using size 3 (3.25mm) needles and A, cast on 52 sts loosely.
Starting with a K row, work in St st for 2 rows.
Now work beaded stripe patt as follows:
Cut off A and join in B.
Row 1 (RS) Knit.
Row 2 Purl.
Row 3 [K7, bead 1] 6 times, K4.
(**Note:** On the rows following the rows the beads have been placed on, purl the stitches behind the beads firmly to encourage the beads to remain at the front of the work.)
Row 4 Purl.
Rows 5 and 6 Rep rows 1 and 2.
Row 7 K3, [bead 1, K7] 6 times, K1.
Row 8 Purl.
Cut off B and join in A.
Row 9 Knit.
Row 10 Purl.
Rows 11–14 [Rep rows 9 and 10] twice.
These 14 rows form beaded stripe patt.
Work in beaded stripe patt until there is insufficient of B to work another beaded stripe, ending after 2 rows using A and with RS facing for next row. Bind off loosely.

Finishing
FELTING
Machine wash completed Scarf at 140°F (60°C) on a full cycle with maximum spin, using laundry detergent but no

fabric conditioner. Once Scarf has been washed, remove any stray fluff and ensure that all beads are sitting on right side of work, gently easing any that may have moved back through the knitting. Gently ease Scarf into shape. Leave to dry naturally with right side up.

Next, add one of following ruffles to each end of Scarf.

Beaded ruffles (both alike)

Thread beads onto A (see opposite page).

With RS facing, using size 3 (3.25mm) needles and A, pick up and knit 50 sts evenly along cast-on (or bound-off) edge of felted Scarf.

Row 1 and every foll alt row Purl.

Row 2 (RS) Inc once in each st to end. *100 sts.*

Row 4 *K1, inc in next st; rep from * to end. *150 sts.*

Row 6 *K1, inc in next st, bead 1, inc in next st, K1, inc in next st; rep from * to end. *225 sts.*

Bind off loosely.

Beaded ruffles with picot edge (both alike)

Thread beads onto A (see opposite page).

With RS facing, using size 3 (3.25mm) needles and A, pick up and knit 50 sts evenly along cast-on (or bound-off) edge of felted Scarf.

Row 1 and every foll alt row Purl.

Row 2 (RS) *K1, inc in next st; rep from * to end. *75 sts.*

Row 4 K1, *inc in next st, K1; rep from * to end. *112 sts.*

Row 6 *K1, inc in next st; rep from * to end. *168 sts.*

Row 8 Rep row 6. *252 sts.*

Row 10 K5, *bead 1, K7; rep from * to last 7 sts, bead 1, K6.

Row 12 Rep row 6. *378 sts.*

Row 13 Purl.

Now work picot bind-off as follows: *cast on 3 sts onto left-hand needle, bind off 6 sts, slip st on right needle back onto left needle; rep from * to end, fastening off last st.

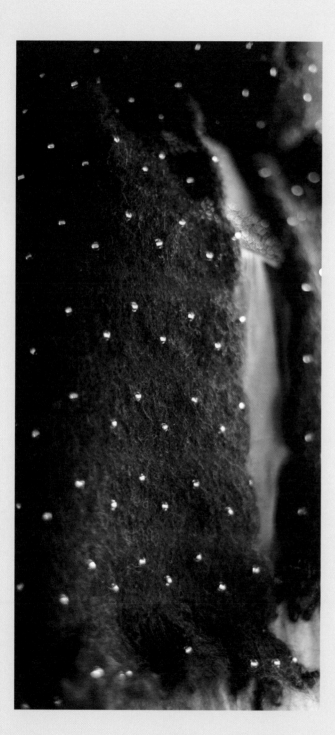

threading beads

When knitting-in beads, you must thread the beads onto the yarn before you begin to knit. Always test this threading technique on the chosen bead to make sure the bead hole is large enough for the yarn you are using. To thread the beads, first thread an ordinary sewing needle with a short length of sewing thread and knot the ends together firmly to form a loop. Next, hang the tail-end of the yarn through the thread loop. Then pick up a bead with the tip of the needle, and push the bead down the needle, over the thread, and onto the yarn. Keep adding beads in this way until you have a sufficient number of beads on the ball of yarn; for example, if you are using three balls of yarn, thread a third of the beads specified onto each ball.

sheer wrap

Finished size
Completed wrap measures approximately 13¾" (35cm) wide by 94½" (240cm) long.

Yarn
8 x ⁷⁄₈oz (25g) balls of Rowan *Scottish Tweed 4-Ply* in **A** (Sunset 011)
3 x ⁷⁄₈oz (25g) balls of Rowan *Kidsilk Haze* in **B** (Marmalade 596)

Needles
Size 3 (3.25mm) circular knitting needle, at least 39½" (100cm) long

Gauge before felting
26 sts and 38 rows to 4" (10cm) measured over stockinette stitch using A and size 3 (3.25mm) needles *or size necessary to obtain correct gauge.*

Abbreviations
See page 109.

Special note
This wrap is knitted sideways on a long circular needle, so its length is governed by the number of stitches you cast on. For a shorter wrap, cast on fewer stitches.
You can carry the *Kidsilk Haze* yarn up the side of the work from stripe to stripe, loosely twisting the two yarns together at the end of the row—this reduces the number of ends to weave in. But do not carry the *Scottish Tweed 4-Ply* from stripe to stripe because it will shrink when felted.
If you would like to add on one of the ruffles on page 16, pick up stitches along the row-ends after the wrap has been felted.

Wrap

Using size 3 (3.25mm) circular needle and A,
cast on 550 sts.
Starting with a K row, work in St st for 8 rows.
Now work in striped St st as follows:
Cut off A and join in B.
Using B, work 6 rows.
Cut off B and join in A.
Using A, work 6 rows.
These 12 rows form striped St st.
Work in striped St st for 132 rows more, ending
after 6 rows using A.
Work 2 rows more using A, ending with RS
facing for next row.
Bind off.

Finishing

FELTING

Machine wash completed Wrap at 140°F (60°C)
on a full cycle with maximum spin, using
laundry detergent but no fabric conditioner.
Once Wrap has been washed, remove any stray
fluff and gently ease it into shape. Leave to dry
naturally with right side up.

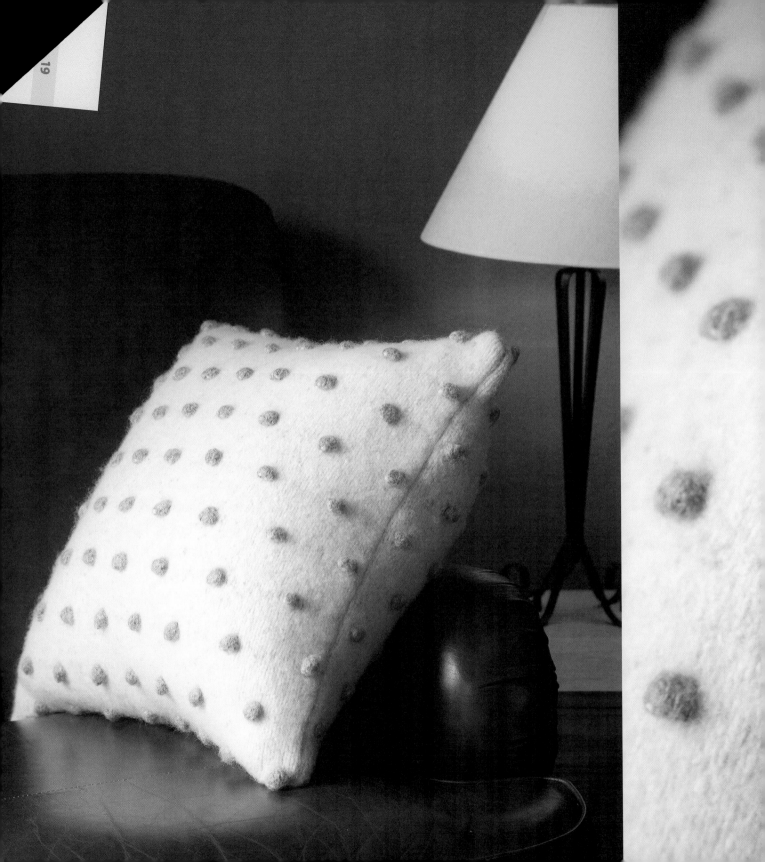

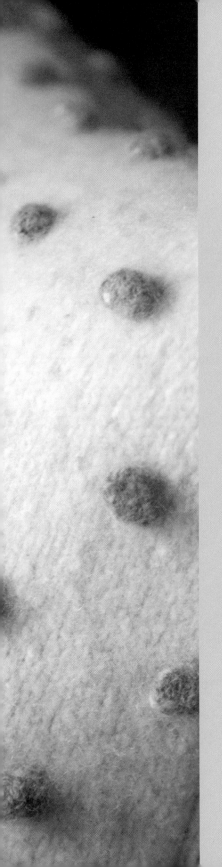

bobble cushion

Large, classic, and very comforting, this cushion is knitted in Rowan *Scottish Tweed Aran*, which felts beautifully to produce a soft, deep fabric.

I liked the simple effect of making a two-tone cushion in a pair of colorways, but if you are into color you could make the bobbles in different contrasting colors all over, or in one color on one side and another on the other side.

The knitted-in bobbles, which are inspired by Shibori textures, are totally transformed by the felting process, which makes them soft but surpisingly effective.

Finished size

Completed cover fits a 19" (48cm) square pillow form.

Yarn

5 x 3½oz (100g) balls of Rowan *Scottish Tweed Aran* in **A**
(Porridge 024 or Claret 013) and 1 ball in **B** (Machair 002 or
Lovat 033)

Needles

Pair of size 8 (5mm) knitting needles

Notions

18" (46cm) zipper

Gauge before felting

16 sts and 23 rows to 4" (10cm) measured over stockinette
stitch using size 8 (5mm) needles *or size necessary to obtain
correct gauge.*

Abbreviations

MB (make bobble) = [K1, P1, K1, P1, K1] all into next st, turn,
P5, turn, K5, turn, P2tog, P1, P2tog, turn, sl 1, K2tog, psso.
See also page 109.

Special note

Because the bobbles are worked in a different color than
the rest of the row, strand the bobble yarn loosely across
the wrong side of the work from one bobble to the next,
weaving it into the wrong side of the work every 3 or 4
stitches. Ensure that the main color is taken tightly across
the back of the bobble so that the bobble stands out from
the knitting.

However, if your are using a light color for the background
and a dark color for the bobbles, use a separate length of
yarn for each bobble—otherwise the stranded bobble yarn
might show through to the front once the piece is felted.

Sides (make 2)

Using size 8 (5mm) needles and A, cast on 100 sts.
Starting with a K row, work in St st for 6 rows, ending with
RS facing for next row.
Join in B.
Row 7 (RS) K4 with A, *MB with B, K1 tbl with A, K10 with A;
rep from * to end.
Cut off B.
Using A, cont in St st for 13 rows, ending with RS facing for
next row.
Join in B.
Row 21 (RS) K10 with A, *MB with B, K1 tbl with A, K10 with A;
rep from * to last 6 sts, MB with B, K1 tbl with A, K4 with A.
Cut off B.
Using A, cont in St st for 13 rows.
Last 28 rows form bobble patt.
Work in bobble patt for 106 rows more, ending after
7 rows using A after 10th bobble row and with RS facing
for next row.
Bind off.

Finishing

FELTING

Machine wash completed Sides at 140°F (60°C) on a full
cycle with maximum spin, using laundry detergent but no
fabric conditioner.
Once Sides have been washed, remove any stray fluff and
gently ease them into shape. Leave to dry naturally with
right side up.

SEAMS

Matching pattern, sew together Sides along three edges
using a sharp-pointed needle. Sew zipper into an opening
along fourth edge.

pleated scarf and corsages

This short, felted scarf, with subtle beads knitted into the fabric, is intended to be worn over a coat or jacket and fastened with a brooch or with one of the corsages (pages 30–33).

Pleats are stitched in place with shrink-resistant thread on the scarf before felting, to create a gentle gathered effect all over the fabric. After felting, the scarf is left to dry and then the stitching is removed. The stitches form a resist against the felting process, thus leaving the undulations in the knitting with some of the individual knitted stitches still visible.

I have made the scarf in two different colors that go well with the corsages, but you can choose any one of many colors.

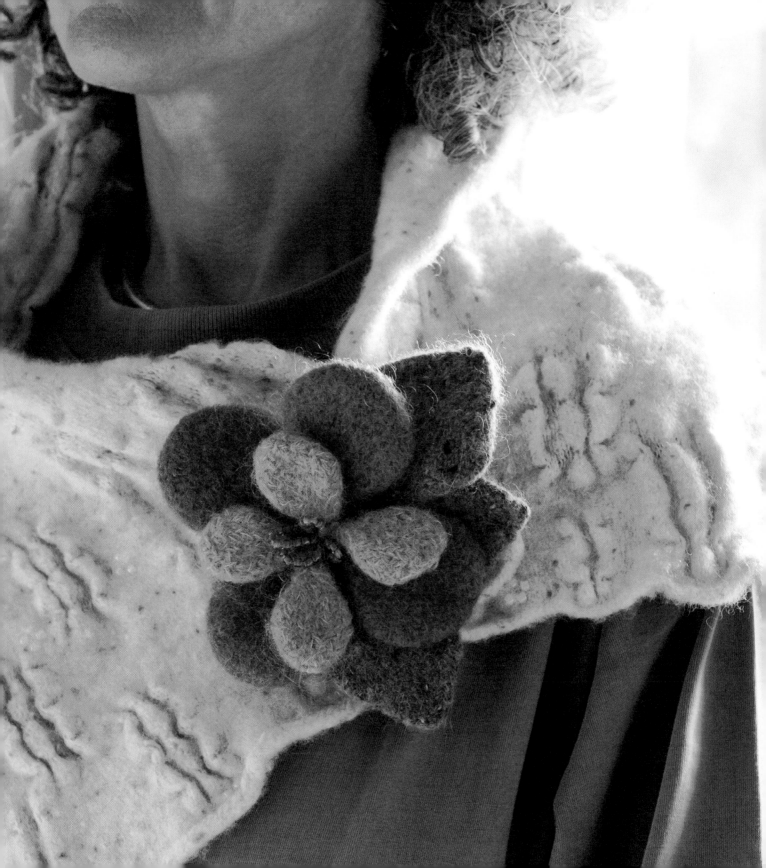

pleated scarf

Finished size

Completed scarf measures approximately 8½" (22cm) wide by 34" (86cm) long.

Yarn

6 x ⅞oz (25g) balls of Rowan *Scottish Tweed 4-Ply* (Porridge 024 or Rust 009)

Needles

Pair of size 3 (3.25mm) knitting needles

Notions

Approximately 130 white or bronze 4mm glass beads
Shrink-resistant thread (such as Anchor six-strand cotton embroidery floss), for making pleats
Decorative brooch or corsage, for fastening

Gauge before felting

26 sts and 38 rows to 4" (10cm) measured over stockinette stitch using size 3 (3.25mm) needles *or size necessary to obtain correct gauge.*

Abbreviations

bead 1 = bring yarn to front (RS) of work between two needles, slide bead up next to st just worked, slip next stitch purlwise from left needle to right needle and take yarn back (WS) of work between two needles leaving bead sitting on RS of work in front of slipped st.
See also page 109.

Scarf

Thread beads onto yarn (see page 17).
Using size 3 (3.25mm) needles, cast on 90 sts.
Starting with a K row, work in St st for 4 rows, ending with RS facing for next row.
Now work in beaded patt as follows:
Row 1 (RS) K13, bead 1, [K20, bead 1] 3 times, K13.
(**Note:** On the rows following the rows the beads have been placed on, purl the stitches behind the beads firmly to encourage the beads to remain at the front of the work.)
Row 2 Purl.
Row 3 K12, [bead 1, K1, bead 1, K18] 3 times, bead 1, K1, bead 1, K12.
Row 4 Purl.
Row 5 Rep row 1.
Starting with a P row, work in St st for 35 rows, ending with RS facing for next row.
Row 41 (RS) K23, bead 1, [K20, bead 1] twice, K24.
Row 42 Purl.
Row 43 K22, [bead 1, K1, bead 1, K18] twice, bead 1, K1, bead 1, K23.
Row 44 Purl.
Row 45 Rep row 41.
Starting with a P row, work in St st for 35 rows, ending with RS facing for next row.
Last 80 rows form beaded patt.
Work in beaded patt for 250 rows more, ending after patt row 10 and with RS facing for next row.
Bind off.

Finishing

EMBELLISHMENT

Using photograph as a guide and following instructions on pages 28–29, sew pleats in place at random along length of Scarf, avoiding beaded areas.

FELTING

Machine wash completed Scarf at 140°F (60°C) on a full cycle with maximum spin, using laundry detergent but no fabric conditioner.

Once Scarf has been washed, remove any stray fluff and ensure that all beads are sitting on right side of work, gently easing any that may have moved back through the knitting. Gently ease Scarf into shape. Leave to dry naturally with right side up. Once dry, remove threads holding pleats in place and remove thread. Fasten Scarf at front with decorative brooch or corsage as shown.

felted pleats

The pleating on knitted felt is sewn in place before the knitting is felted, using shrink-resistant thread that will not felt (Anchor six-strand cotton embroidery floss or Rowan *4-Ply Cotton* yarn are ideal). The thread holds the knitting tightly together, and once it goes into the washing machine, the area inside the pleats cannot felt. The thread is only removed when the knitting is fully dry.

You can achieve different effects with the same pleating technique. If you pleat with the right side facing up, the indents create furrows on the right side of the felted fabric. If you pleat with the wrong side facing up, the indents create protrusions on the right side of the fabric.

On some designs in this book, the felted pleating is random, such as on the Pleated Scarf on pages 24–27. On others, the pleating is regular and uniform, such as on the Striped Scarf on pages 76–79. You can vary the pleat positions, the number of folds, and the number of holding stitches. The most important thing is to sew the pleats very firmly and to secure the thread ends firmly so they don't come undone in the washing machine.

Pleating the unfelted knitting

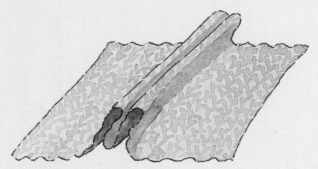

1 Pinch the fabric together to form either two or three folded pleats.

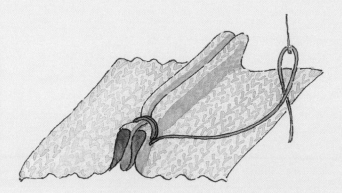

2 Using the shrink-resistant thread and a blunt-ended yarn needle, pierce through all the layers of the pleats, inserting the needle at one side and bringing it out at the other side as shown above. Work three stitches in the same place, pulling the thread firmly each time. Then firmly secure the thread end.

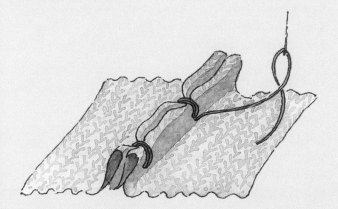

3 Make another stitch the same about 2" (5cm) up or down from the first holding stitch. Now make a third, in the center between the first two. (Your instructions will sometimes tell you how far apart to position these holding stitches.) Continue making as many holding stitches as required along the pleat.

4 Repeat the pleats in the same way all over the knitting as instructed, positioning them in uniform positions or at random as required.

5 When all the required pleating is in place, wash the knitting in the washing machine following the instructions in the knitting pattern. After the washing process, leave the item to dry out completely.

6 When the felted knitting is completely dry, very carefully snip out and pull free the shrink-resistant threads used for the pleating. Be careful not to nick the fabric, which will be unfelted in this area and will therefore unravel if you cut it.

diana corsage

Finished size
Completed corsage measures approximately 4" (10cm) in diameter, excluding leaves.

Yarn
1 x 1¾oz (50g) ball of Rowan *Kid Classic* in each of **A** (Lavender Ice 841) and **B** (Tea Rose 854)
1 x 1¾oz (50g) ball of Rowan *Felted Tweed* in **C** (Herb 146)

Needles
Pair of size 6 (4mm) knitting needles
Pair of size 8 (5mm) knitting needles

Notions
Approximately 35 blue 4mm glass beads
Brooch back or safety pin, for fastening corsage

Gauge before felting
19 sts and 25 rows to 4" (10cm) measured over stockinette stitch using A and size 8 (5mm) needles *or size necessary to obtain correct gauge.*

Abbreviations
See page 109.

Base
Using size 8 (5mm) needles and A, cast on 10 sts.
Work in garter st (knit every row) for 2 rows, ending with RS facing for next row.
Row 3 (RS) K1, M1, K to last st, M1, K1.
Cont in garter st throughout and working all increases as set by last row, work in garter st, inc 1 st at each end of 2nd row and foll 6 alt rows. *26 sts.*
Work even until Base measures 1³/8" (3.5cm) from last inc,

ending with RS facing for next row.
Next row (RS) K1, K2tog, K to last 3 sts, K2tog tbl, K1.
Working all decreases as set by last row, dec 1 st at each end of 2nd row and foll 6 alt rows. *10 sts.*
Work 1 row.
Bind off.

Leaves (make 3)
Using size 6 (4mm) needles and C, cast on 3 sts.
Row 1 (RS) K1, inc in next st, K1. *4 sts.*
Row 2 Purl.
Row 3 K1, M1, K to last st, M1, K1.
Rows 4–13 [Rep rows 2 and 3] 5 times. *16 sts.*
Row 14 Purl.
Row 15 Knit.
Row 16 Purl.
Row 17 K1, K2tog, K to last 3 sts, K2tog tbl, K1.
Rows 18–27 [Rep rows 16 and 17] 5 times. *4 sts.*
Row 28 [P2tog] twice.
Bind off rem 2 sts.

Large petals (make 4)
Using size 8 (5mm) needles and B, cast on 6 sts.
Row 1 (RS) Inc in first st, K3, inc in next st, K1. *8 sts.*
Row 2 Purl.
Row 3 K1, M1, K to last st, M1, K1.
Rows 4–9 [Rep rows 2 and 3] 3 times. *16 sts.*
Row 10 Purl.
Row 11 Knit.
Row 12 Purl.
Row 13 K1, K2tog, K to last 3 sts, K2tog tbl, K1.
Rows 14–21 [Rep rows 12 and 13] 4 times. *6 sts.*
Row 22 P2, P2tog, P2. *5 sts.*
Row 23 K1, sl 1, K2tog, psso, K1.
Bind off rem 3 sts.

Small petals (make 4)

Using size 8 (5mm) needles and A, cast on 3 sts.

Row 1 (RS) K1, inc in next st, K1. *4 sts.*

Row 2 Purl.

Row 3 K1, M1, K to last st, M1, K1.

Rows 4–7 [Rep rows 2 and 3] twice. *10 sts.*

Row 8 Purl.

Row 9 K1, K2tog, K to last 3 sts, K2tog tbl, K1.

Rows 10–13 [Rep rows 8 and 9] twice. *4 sts.*

Bind off rem 4 sts.

Finishing

FELTING

Machine wash all pieces at 104°F (40°C) on a full cycle with maximum spin, using laundry detergent but no fabric conditioner; add an old towel to the machine to increase the agitation.

Once pieces have been washed, remove any stray fluff and ease them gently into shape. Leave to dry naturally.

ASSEMBLY

Using photograph as a guide, position Leaves on Base and sew in place using a sharp-pointed needle. Arrange Large Petals on top of Leaves, then Small Petals on top of these, and sew all Petals to Base.

BEAD STAMENS

Make four strings of beads of varying lengths, form into loops, and sew to center of Corsage as shown.

Sew brooch back (or safety pin) to back of Corsage.

hester corsage

Finished size
Completed corsage is approximately 5" (13cm) in diameter, including leaves.

Yarn
1 x ⅞oz (25g) ball of Rowan *Scottish Tweed 4-Ply* in each of **A** (Brilliant Pink 010) and **B** (Thistle 016)

1 x ⅞oz (25g) ball of Rowan *Kidsilk Haze* in **C** (Violetta 633)

Needles
Pair of size 3 (3.25mm) knitting needles

Notions
Approximately 50 mauve 3mm matte glass beads
Brooch back or safety pin, for fastening corsage

Gauge before felting
26 sts and 38 rows to 4" (10cm) measured over stockinette stitch using A and size 3 (3.25mm) needles *or size necessary to obtain correct gauge.*

Abbreviations
See page 109.

Flowers (make 2)
Using size 3 (3.25mm) needles and A, cast on 1 st loosely.

Row 1 (WS) K into front, back, front, back, front, and back again of the one cast-on st. *6 sts.*

Shape first petal

Row 2 (RS) K1 and turn, leaving rem 5 sts on a holder (for other 5 petals).

Row 3 Inc purlwise in st. *2 sts.*

Row 4 K1, inc in last st. *3 sts.*

Row 5 Purl.

Row 6 K1, inc once in each of next 2 sts. *5 sts.*

Row 7 Purl.

Row 8 K1, [inc in next st, K1] twice. *7 sts.*

Row 9 Purl.

Row 10 K2, inc in next st, K1, inc in next st, K2. *9 sts.*

Starting with a P row, work in St st for 9 rows, ending with RS facing for next row.

Cont in St st throughout, dec 1 st at each end of next row and foll 2 alt rows. *3 sts.*

Work 1 row.

Row 26 (RS) K2tog, K1.

Row 27 P2.

Row 28 K2tog and fasten off.

Shape remaining petals

Return to sts left on holder, rejoin yarn with RS facing and work rows 2 to 28 again. Cont in this way until 6 petals have been worked and all original 6 sts used up. Make another Flower in exactly the same way but using B.

Outer petals (make 5)
Using size 3 (3.25mm) needles and C, cast on 1 st.

Row 1 (RS) K into front and back of the one cast-on st. *2 sts.*

Row 2 Inc purlwise in each st. *4 sts.*

Row 3 K1, inc once in each of next 2 sts, K1. *6 sts.*

Row 4 P1, M1, P to last st, M1, P1.

Row 5 K1, M1, K to last st, M1, K1.

Rows 6–9 [Rep rows 4 and 5] twice.

Row 10 Rep row 4. *20 sts.*

Starting with a K row, work in St st for 4 rows, ending with RS facing for next row.

Row 15 (RS) K1, K2tog, K to last 3 sts, K2tog tbl, K1.

Row 16 P1, P2tog tbl, P to last 3 sts, P2tog, P1.

Rows 17–22 [Rep rows 15 and 16] 3 times. *4 sts.*

Row 23 K1, K2tog, K1.

Row 24 P3tog and fasten off.

Flower center

Using size 3 (3.25mm) needles and C, cast on 60 sts loosely.
Row 1 (RS) [K2tog] 30 times. *30 sts.*
Row 2 Knit.
Row 3 [K2tog] 15 times. *15 sts.*
Row 4 Knit.
Row 5 [K1, K2tog] 5 times.
Cut off yarn and thread through rem 10 sts. Pull up tight
and fasten off securely.

Finishing

EMBELLISHMENT

Using a blunt-ended yarn needle and B, embroider a
line of backstitches down center of each flower
petal on Flower knitted in A.

FELTING

Machine wash the Flowers ONLY
at 140°F (60°C) on a full cycle
with maximum spin, using
laundry detergent but no
fabric conditioner; add an
old towel to the machine
to increase the agitation.
Once Flowers have been
washed, remove any stray
fluff and gently ease them into
shape. Leave to dry naturally.

ASSEMBLY

Lay one Flower on top of the other Flower
so that petals of one Flower sit between
petals of other Flower. Sew together
at center using a sharp-pointed needle.
Sew Outer Petals in place behind Flowers,
and sew a bead to tip of each of these
Petals. Sew Flower Center in place at center
of Flowers.

BEAD STAMENS

Make two strings of beads—one of about 25 beads and one
of about 20 beads. Form into loops and attach securely to
center of Flower Center as in photograph.
Sew brooch back (or safety pin) to back of Corsage.

beaded scarf

A thick and warm scarf, this felted knit has the same "bumps" as the bag on page 46 and is also beaded. Knitted in Rowan *Kid Classic*, it yields a fairly heavy fabric after felting, reminiscent of astrakhan or bouclé materials.

The pearl beads arranged in a diamond pattern are knitted-in. Created using marbles tied into the prefelted knitting, the "bumps" give a modern twist and some interesting texture to the scarf.

Fasten it with a classic brooch, handmade charm pin, or corsage to complete your individual look.

Finished size

Completed scarf measures approximately 8½" (22cm) wide by 36¼" (92cm) long.

Yarn

5 x 1¾oz (50g) balls of Rowan *Kid Classic* (Crystal 840)

Needles

Pair of size 10½ (6.5mm) knitting needles

Notions

Approximately 330 white 4mm glass beads
14 marbles 15mm in diameter, for creating the "bumps"
Shrink-resistant thread (such as Anchor six-strand cotton embroidery floss), for tying marbles in place
Decorative brooch or charm pin, for fastening

Gauge before felting

17 sts and 20 rows to 4" (10cm) measured over stockinette stitch using size 10½ (6.5mm) needles *or size necessary to obtain correct gauge*.

Abbreviations

bead 1 = bring yarn to front (RS) of work between two needles, slide bead up next to st just worked, slip next stitch purlwise from left needle to right needle and take yarn back (WS) of work between two needles leaving bead sitting on RS of work in front of slipped st.
See also page 109.

Scarf

Thread half the beads onto first ball of yarn (see page 17).
Using size 10½ (6.5mm) needles, cast on 61 sts.
Work 2 rows in garter st (knit every row).
Now work beaded border patt as follows:
Row 1 (RS) K2, bead 1, [K13, bead 1] 4 times, K2.

(**Note:** On the rows following the rows the beads have been placed on, purl the stitches behind the beads firmly to encourage the beads to remain at the front of the work.)
Row 2 and every foll alt row K2, P to last 2 sts, K2.
Row 3 K3, [bead 1, K11, bead 1, K1] 4 times, K2.
Row 5 K3, [K1, bead 1, K9, bead 1, K2] 4 times, K2.
Row 7 K3, [K2, bead 1, K7, bead 1, K3] 4 times, K2.
Row 9 K3, [K3, bead 1, K5, bead 1, K4] 4 times, K2.
Row 11 K3, [K4, bead 1, K3, bead 1, K5] 4 times, K2.
Row 13 K3, [K5, bead 1, K1, bead 1, K6] 4 times, K2.
Row 15 K3, [K6, bead 1, K7] 4 times, K2.
Row 17 Rep row 13.
Row 19 Rep row 11.
Row 21 Rep row 9.
Row 23 Rep row 7.
Row 25 Rep row 5.
Row 27 Rep row 3.
Row 28 Rep row 2.
These 28 rows form beaded border patt.
Work in patt for 15 rows more, ending after patt row 15 and with WS facing for next row.
This completes beaded border.
Next row (WS) K2, P to last 2 sts, K2.
Next row Knit.
Rep last 2 rows until approximately three quarters of last ball of yarn remains, ending with RS facing for next row.
Cut off yarn, thread other half of beads onto yarn, and rejoin yarn.
Starting with patt row 15, work in beaded border patt for 43 rows, ending after a patt row 1 and with WS facing for next row.
Next row Knit.
Rep last row once more.
Bind off.

Finishing

EMBELLISHMENT

Using photograph as a guide and following instructions on page 50, position a marble in center of each diamond of beaded border patt and tie in place with shrink-resistant thread.

FELTING

Machine wash completed Scarf at 104°F (40°C) on a full cycle with maximum spin, using laundry detergent but no fabric conditioner. After washing, take Scarf out of the machine and immediately remove threads holding marbles in place, then remove marbles. Next, remove any stray fluff and ensure that all beads are sitting on right side of work, gently easing any that may have moved back through the knitting. Gently ease Scarf into shape—this may be tricky as the fabric will be very stiff.

While Scarf is still damp, fold down "collar" section into position it will be when worn; if left to dry in this position, it will hold its shape. Leave to dry naturally with right side up.

Fasten Scarf at front with decorative brooch or charm pin as shown.

daisy bag

Strong, yet also really pretty, this versatile stripy bucket bag in Rowan *Scottish Tweed Aran* is a generous size. But it could easily be sized up or down using felting principles (see pages 104–109.)

The bag is decorated with simple embroidered lazy daisy stitches and French knots before it is felted. The braided, felted strap sports really pretty petaled flowers, in softly toning colors of Rowan *Scottish Tweed 4-Ply*. Why not make these flowers individually for felted brooches?

Finished size

Completed bag measures approximately 13½" (34cm) wide at top, 7¾" (20cm) wide at base, and 13½" (34cm) tall, excluding straps.

Yarn

2 x 3½oz (100g) balls of Rowan *Scottish Tweed Aran* in each of **A** (Porridge 024) and **B** (Machair 002)

1 x ⅞oz (25g) ball of Rowan *Scottish Tweed 4-Ply* in each of **C** (Brilliant Pink 010), **D** (Claret 013), **E** (Gold 028), **F** (Sunset 011), and **G** (Lavender 005)

Needles

Pair of size 3 (3.25mm) knitting needles
Pair of size 8 (5mm) knitting needles

Gauge before felting

16 sts and 23 rows to 4" (10cm) measured over stockinette stitch using A and size 8 (5mm) needles *or size necessary to obtain correct gauge.*

Abbreviations

See page 109.

Special note

As many strong contrasting colors are used for this bag, it is a good idea to add a sheet of Color Catcher™ to the washing machine when felting to prevent the colors from running.

Sides (make 2)

Using size 8 (5mm) needles and A, cast on 70 sts.
Starting with a K row, work in St st for 17 rows, ending with WS facing for next row.
Row 18 (WS) Knit (to form fold line).
Starting with a K row, work in St st for 18 rows, ending with RS facing for next row.

Cut off A and join in B.
Cont in St st throughout, dec 1 st at each end of 7th row and 3 foll 6th rows. *62 sts.*
Work 5 rows.
Cut off B and join in A.
Dec 1 st at each end of next row and 4 foll 6th rows. *52 sts.*
Work 5 rows.
Cut off A and join in B.
Dec 1 st at each end of next row and 4 foll 6th rows. *42 sts.*
Work 5 rows, ending with RS facing for next row. Bind off.

Base

Using size 8 (5mm) needles and B, cast on 30 sts.
Starting with a K row, work in St st, inc 1 st at each end of 3rd row and foll 5 alt rows. *42 sts.*
Cont in St st throughout, work 3 rows, ending with RS facing for next row.
Dec 1 st at each end of next row and foll 5 alt rows. *30 sts.*
Work 1 row, ending with RS facing for next row. Bind off.

Flowers (make 6)

Using size 3 (3.25mm) needles and D, cast on 96 sts.
Row 1 (RS) Knit.
Cut off D and join in C.
Row 2 and every foll alt row Purl.
Row 3 [K4, K2tog] 16 times. *80 sts.*
Row 5 [K3, K2tog] 16 times. *64 sts.*
Row 7 [K2, K2tog] 16 times. *48 sts.*
Row 9 [K1, K2tog] 16 times.
Cut off yarn and thread through rem 32 sts. Pull up tight and fasten off securely.

Finishing

STRAP

Cut 20 lengths of A and 10 lengths of B, each 94½" (240cm) long. Using 10 lengths of same color yarn for each group, braid these 30 lengths together and knot ends, leaving a tassel about 1½–2" (4–5cm) long at each end.

EMBELLISHMENT

Using a blunt-ended yarn needle and C, D, E, F, and G, embroider flowers on Sides as shown. For each flower, work 5–7 lazy daisy stitches, or many straight stitches radiating out from one point.

Using four strands of a contrasting color, embroider a large French knot or a group of small French knots at the center of each flower. If desired, sprinkle a few large French knots around the flowers.

BAG SEAMS

Using a blunt-ended yarn needle, sew Sides of Bag together along row-end edges. Matching center of row-end edges of Base to side seams, sew Base to bound-off edges of Sides. Fold first 17 rows to inside along fold-line row around top of bag and slip-stitch in place.

FELTING

Machine wash completed Bag, Strap, and Flowers at 140°F (60°C) on a full cycle with maximum spin, using laundry detergent but no fabric conditioner; add an old towel to the machine to ensure adequate agitation.

Once pieces have been washed, remove any stray fluff and gently ease them into their correct shapes. Leave to dry naturally with right side up.

STRAP AND FLOWERS

Using a sharp-pointed needle, sew Strap to outside of bag along side seams. Sew three Flowers to each end of Strap.

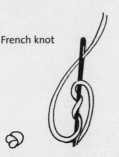

French knot

Lazy daisy stitch

leafy place mats and coasters

Subtle and minimalist, these felted place mats are really solid, and thick enough to protect any table from plates and mugs.

I chose to create them in Rowan *Scottish Tweed DK*, and decorated them with a simple two–tone leaf pattern in chain stitch. The leaf shapes on the mats are outlined with sparkly beads, as is the outer edge of each mat. As usual, felting works its magic on the embroidery and beads, gently embedding them in the fabric.

Worked in the reverse colorway, the matching set of coasters completes the ensemble.

place mats

Finished size
Each completed place mat measures approximately
21" (53cm) wide by 12" (30cm) tall.

Yarn
8 x 1¾oz (50g) balls of Rowan *Scottish Tweed DK* in **A** (Lewis
Grey 007) and small amount in each of **B** (Grey Mist 001)
and **C** (Midnight 023), for embroidery

Needles
Pair of size 6 (4mm) knitting needles

Notions
Approximately 750 crystal 4mm glass beads

Gauge before felting
21 sts and 29 rows to 4" (10cm) measured over stockinette
stitch using size 6 (4mm) needles *or size necessary to
obtain correct gauge.*

Abbreviations
See page 109.

Special note
As the beads are sewn on with a yarn that will shrink and
felt, they will felt securely in place. If you find it difficult
to sew on the beads with yarn A, use the same shade in
Rowan *Scottish Tweed 4-Ply* instead.

Place mats (make 4)
Using size 6 (4mm) needles and A, cast on 110 sts.
Starting with a K row, work in St st for 100 rows, ending
with RS facing for next row.
Bind off.

Finishing
EMBELLISHMENT
Using a blunt-ended yarn needle and B, embroider two sets
of three leaves in corner of each mat in chain stitch as
shown (use template on page 110 for leaf shape). Using C,
embroider chain-stitch veins in center of each leaf.
Using a blunt-ended yarn needle and A (see Special Note),
sew on beads along one outer edge of two leaves of each
group, and around entire outer edge of place mat—place
beads approximately ³⁄₈" (1cm) apart and ³⁄₈" (1cm) in from
outer edge of mat.
FELTING
Machine wash completed Place Mats at 140°F (60°C) on a
full cycle with maximum spin, using laundry detergent but
no fabric conditioner.
Once Place Mats have been washed, remove any stray fluff
and ensure that all beads are sitting on right side of mat,
gently easing any that may have moved back through
the knitting.
Gently ease Place Mats into shape—cast-on and bound-off
edges may curl slightly. Leave to dry naturally with right
side up.

coasters

Finished size
Completed coaster measures approximately 4¼" (11cm)
in diameter.

Yarn
1 x 1¾oz (50g) ball of Rowan *Scottish Tweed DK* in **A** (Grey
Mist 001) and small amount in B (Lewis Grey 007), for
embroidery
Note: One ball of A is enough to make 3–4 coasters.

Needles
Pair of size 6 (4mm) knitting needles

Notions
Approximately 44 black 4mm black glass beads for each coaster

Gauge before felting
Same as for Place Mats.

Abbreviations
See page 109.

Coaster
Using size 6 (4mm) needles and A, cast on 10 sts.
Work 4 rows in garter st (knit every row), inc 1 st at each end of every row. *18 sts.*
Cont in garter st throughout, work 1 row.
Inc 1 st at each end of next row and 3 foll alt rows. *26 sts.*
Work 3 rows.
Inc 1 st at each end of next row. *28 sts.*
Work for 3¼" (8cm) more.
Dec 1 st at each end of next row. *26 sts.*
Work 3 rows.
Dec 1 st at each end of next row and 3 foll alt rows. *18 sts.*
Dec 1 st at each end of next 4 rows. *10 sts.*
Bind off.

Finishing

EMBELLISHMENT
Using a blunt-ended yarn needle and B, embroider two overlapping leaves on each coaster in chain stitch as shown (use template on page 110 for leaf shape). Using B, embroider chain-stitch veins in center of each leaf.
Using a blunt-ended yarn needle and A (see Special Note for Place Mats on opposite page), sew on beads around entire outer edge of each coaster—place beads approximately ³/₈" (1cm) apart and ³/₈" (1cm) in from outer edge of coaster.

FELTING
Wash and dry as for Place Mats on opposite page, but because these are small items, add an old towel to the wash for extra agitation.

Chain stitch

"bump" striped bag

This unusual felted bag is ideal as a knitting or craft-project bag. It is worked in Rowan *Scottish Tweed Aran* yarn, and then washed in the machine to felt it. The resulting felt is very stable and durable, so the bag doesn't need a fabric lining.

The "bumps" are felted in, using marbles that you tie in before washing. After you remove the marbles, once the felting is complete, the fabric retains the raised "bumps" they made.

For extra interest, the surface of the knitting is embroidered with chain stitches. Because the embroidery almost "melts" in the felting process, you get very attractive soft lines of color rather than hard contrasts.

Finished size
Completed bag measures approximately 17½" (45cm) wide, 11" (28cm) tall (excluding handles), and 5½" (14cm) deep.

Yarn
2 x 3½oz (100g) balls of Rowan *Scottish Tweed Aran* in **A** (Storm Grey 004), 3 balls in **B** (Midnight 023), and 1 ball in **C** (Porridge 024)

Needles
Pair of size 8 (5mm) knitting needles

Notions
Pair of D-shaped bamboo bag handles, 11¾" (30cm) wide (Rowan ref 00402)
22 marbles 15mm in diameter, for creating the "bumps"
Shrink-resistant thread (such as Anchor six-strand cotton embroidery floss), for tying marbles in place

Gauge before felting
16 sts and 23 rows to 4" (10cm) measured over stockinette stitch using size 8 (5mm) needles *or size necessary to obtain correct gauge.*

Abbreviations
See page 109.

Special note
Washed at the temperature recommended in this pattern for felting, *Scottish Tweed Aran* will shed color, so consider using a sheet of Color Catcher™ in the felting wash.
In order to achieve the required felted size, it may be necessary to wash the bag twice—as was the case with the bag photographed. After the first wash, check the size of the bag and, if necessary, wash again to obtain the correct size, keeping the marbles tied in place.

Sides (make 2)
Using size 8 (5mm) needles and A, cast on 69 sts.
Starting with a K row, work in St st for 14 rows, ending with RS facing for next row.
Row 15 (RS) Purl (to form fold line).
Starting with a P row, work in St st for 13 rows, ending with RS facing for next row.
Cut off A and join in B.
Row 29 (RS) K1, M1, K to last st, M1, K1. *71 sts.*
Mark each end of last row with a cotton thread.
Purl 1 row.
Cut off B and join in C.
Cont in St st throughout and working all increases as set by row 29, inc 1 st at each end of next row and foll 4 alt rows, then on foll 4th row. *83 sts.*
Cut off C and join in B.
Work 2 rows.
Cut off B and join in A.
Work 1 row.
Inc 1 st at each end of next row and 2 foll 4th rows. *89 sts.*
Work 5 rows.
Cut off A and join in B.
Work 2 rows.
Cut off B and join in C.
Work 15 rows.
Cut off C and join in B.
Work even until Side measures 19½" (50cm) from cast-on edge, ending with RS facing for next row. Bind off.

Gusset
Using size 8 (5mm) needles and B, cast on 26 sts.
Starting with a K row, work in St st until Gusset, unstretched and starting and ending at markers, fits down one row-end edge to bound-off edge, across bound-off edge, and then up other row-end edge, ending with RS facing for next row. Bind off.

Pockets (make 2)

Using size 8 (5mm) needles and A, cast on 15 sts.

Starting with a K row, work in St st for 4 rows, ending with RS facing for next row.

Row 5 (RS) K1, M1, K to last st, M1, K1. *17 sts.*

Cont in St st throughout and working all increases as set by last row, inc 1 st at each end of 2nd row and foll 9 alt rows. *37 sts.*

Work even until Pocket measures 6¼" (16cm), ending with RS facing for next row.

Next row (RS) K1, K2tog tbl, K to last 3 sts, K2tog, K1.

Working all decreases as set by last row, dec 1 st at each end of 2nd row. *33 sts.*

Work 1 row, ending with RS facing for next row.

Cut off yarn A and join in yarn B. Bind off.

Finishing

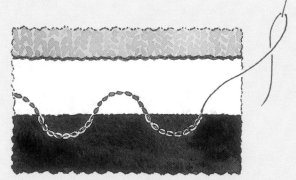

EMBELLISHMENT

Using a blunt-ended yarn needle and A or a combination of B and C, embroider a wavy line of chain stitches across both Sides of Bag (see above), positioning wavy line so that it straddles first and second stripes at bottom of Bag as shown on page 46. If desired, embroider a chain-stitch spiral on each Pocket using B.

Following instructions on page 50 for creating "bumps," position eleven marbles across top two stripes of each Side—five marbles along top stripe and six marbles on next stripe—and tie in place.

SEAMS

Matching cast-on and bound-off edges of Gusset to first row of Sides in B (at markers), sew Gusset to Sides along row-end and bound-off edges using a blunt-ended yarn needle.

FELTING

Machine wash completed Bag and Pockets at 140°F (60°C) (see Special Note) on a full cycle with maximum spin, using laundry detergent but no fabric conditioner. After washing, take pieces out of the machine and immediately remove threads holding marbles in place, then remove marbles. Next, remove any stray fluff and gently ease pieces into their correct shapes. Leave to dry naturally with right side up.

POCKETS AND HANDLES

Using a sharp-pointed needle on felted pieces, sew Pockets (with bound-off edges at top) to inside of Sides of Bag.

Fold first 14 rows of Sides of Bag to inside along fold-line row, insert handles under hem, and sew hem in place.

felted "bumps"

To create "bumps" in some of the felted knitting in this book, I used marbles (or wooden beads) as the resisting objects. The marbles are tied in place, washed with the item, then removed. The knitted fabric felts everywhere except where the fabric has been stretched over the marble. Once the marbles are removed, the shape of the marble is left behind, with the knitted stitches clearly visible on the bumps. Unless the item is felted again, this is now a permanent feature of the fabric.

"Bumps" can be placed in groups, or in lines, depending upon the effect you want. But, because of the distortion, avoid placing them too close together, or too close to the edge on scarves. For more irregular "bumps," you could use pebbles in place of the marbles.

You must use a strong, shrink-resistant thread for tying the marbles, or it will felt into the work and make it very difficult to remove the marbles. Anchor six-strand cotton embroidery floss or Rowan *4-Ply Cotton* yarn is ideal.

Making "bumps"

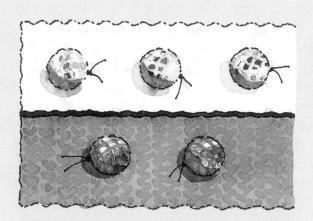

1 Hold the marble on the wrong side of the work and stretch the fabric tightly over it. Wrap the thread firmly around the marble two or three times and double knot it.

2 Secure marbles in place in the same way for all the "bumps" required. For an even, regular effect, you can mark the positions of the marbles with chalk first, because the distortion can make it hard to follow a pattern once you start the tying. The chalk will wash off in the felting. What you see on the marbles once tied in place is what the finished result will look like.

3 Once all the marbles are tied securely in place, wash the item in the washing machine to felt it.

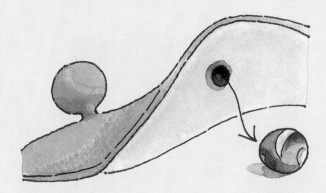

4 Take the item out of the machine and immediately remove the marbles by carefully snipping the threads away and popping them out. Push the "bumps" back into shape by poking your finger inside, and leave the item to dry fully.

rosebud scarf

Bobbles in a toning color are knitted into this scarf, which is then hand-pleated (see pages 28–29) over the bobbles before felting to give a soft but uniform texture. Rowan's *Scottish Tweed 4-Ply* felts down to make a delightfully soft fabric that reveals the unfelted bobbles.

This design would work well as a bigger throw or a lap blanket, too. It would be easy to adapt in size once you have mastered the skills of making felted knitting test swatches as explained on pages 104–109. There's nothing to it!

Finished size

Completed scarf measures approximately 5½" (14cm) wide by 45¼" (115cm) long.

Yarn

6 x ⅞oz (25g) balls of Rowan *Scottish Tweed 4-Ply* in **A** (Porridge 024) and 1 ball in **B** (Rose 026)

Needles

Pair of size 3 (3.25mm) knitting needles

Notions

Shrink-resistant thread (such as Anchor six-strand cotton embroidery floss), for making pleats

Gauge before felting

26 sts and 38 rows to 4" (10cm) measured over stockinette stitch using size 3 (3.25mm) needles *or size necessary to obtain correct gauge*.

Abbreviations

MB (make bobble) = [K1, P1, K1, P1, K1] all into next st, turn, P5, turn, K5, turn, P2tog, P1, P2tog, turn, sl 1, K2tog, psso. See also page 109.

Special note

Because the bobbles are worked in a different color than the rest of the row, strand the bobble yarn loosely across the wrong side of the work from one bobble to the next, weaving it into the wrong side of the work every 3 or 4 stitches. Ensure that the main color is taken tightly across the back of the bobble so that the bobble stands out from the knitting. However, if your are using a light color for the background and a dark color for the bobbles, use a separate length of yarn for each bobble—otherwise the stranded bobble yarn might show through to the front once the piece is felted.

Scarf

Using size 3 (3.25mm) needles and A, cast on 79 sts.
Starting with a K row, work in St st for 10 rows, ending with RS facing for next row.
Now work in bobble patt as follows:
Join in B.
Row 1 (RS) K15 with A, *MB with B, K1 tbl with A, K14 with A; rep from * to end.
Cut off B.
Using A, cont in St st for 17 rows.
Join in B.
Row 19 (RS) K7 with A, *MB with B, K1 tbl with A, K14 with A; rep from * to last 8 sts, MB with B, K1 tbl with A, K6 with A.
Cut off B.
Using A, cont in St st for 17 rows, ending with RS facing for next row.
Last 36 rows form bobble patt.
Work in bobble patt until Scarf measures approximately 59" (150cm), ending after patt row 1 or 9.
Using A, cont in St st for 9 rows more.
Bind off.

Finishing

EMBELLISHMENT

Using photograph as a guide and following instructions on pages 28–29, form a pleat to enclose each bobble and stitch securely in place using shrink-resistant thread.

FELTING

Machine wash completed Scarf at 140°F (60°C) on a full cycle with maximum spin, using laundry detergent but no fabric conditioner.
Once Scarf has been washed, remove any stray fluff and gently ease it into shape. Leave to dry naturally with right side up.
Once dry, remove threads securing pleats so that pleats spring into place revealing unfelted bobbles.

ruffled bag

This medium-size bag gives you the chance to try out a Shibori weaving technique, using unspun fibers, cut into short lengths and woven into the knitted base fabric before felting. It has a handy capacious inner pocket to hold things that you don't want lost in the depths of the bag.

Once the Rowan *Scottish Tweed Aran* of the bag is felted, the woven-in strands are caught in the felt to create a very interesting effect. As a contrast, the double ruffle decorating the top of the bag is knitted on after felting in Rowan's *Kidsilk Haze*.

Finished size

Completed bag measures approximately 17" (43cm) wide and 11¾" (30cm) tall, including ruffle.

Yarn

2 x 3½oz (100g) balls of Rowan *Scottish Tweed Aran* in **A** (Midnight 023) and 1 ball in **B** (Lavender 005)
1 x ⅞oz (25g) ball of Rowan *Kidsilk Haze* in **C** (Violetta 633)

Needles

Pair of size 6 (4mm) knitting needles
Pair of size 8 (5mm) knitting needles (or circular needle if preferred)
Pair of size 9 (5.5mm) knitting needles

Notions

Pair of U-shaped bag handles, 9" (23cm) wide (Rowan ref 00404)
Unspun silk or linen fibers (or shrink-resistant fancy yarns) in contrasting colors
31½" (80cm) of ⅜" (1cm) wide ribbon
One large snap fastener
Shrink-resistant thread (such as Anchor six-strand cotton embroidery floss), for making pleats

Gauge before felting

16 sts and 23 rows to 4" (10cm) measured over stockinette stitch using A and size 9 (5.5mm) needles *or size necessary to obtain correct gauge.*

Abbreviations

See page 109.

Special note

When weaving in the strands of silk or linen fibers, be generous; the effect is best if you don't leave large gaps undecorated. You can use almost anything for the woven-in strands, but remember that some wool yarns will felt and the effect they will create will vary from the bag shown. If in doubt, experiment on the pocket first (see page 60).

Sides (make 2)

Using size 8 (5mm) needles (or circular needle if preferred) and B, cast on 240 sts.
Row 1 (RS) *K2, lift second st on right needle over first st and off right needle (as though binding off 1 st); rep from * to end. *120 sts.*
Row 2 Purl.
Row 3 Rep row 1. *60 sts.*
Starting with a P row, work in St st for 5 rows, ending with RS facing for next row.
Cut off B and join in A.
Change to size 9 (5.5mm) needles.
Starting with a K row and cont in St st throughout, inc 1 st at each end of next row and foll 3 alt rows, then on 3 foll 4th rows, then on 2 foll 6th rows. *78 sts.*
Work even until section in A measures 13" (33cm), ending with RS facing for next row.
Bind off.

Pocket

Using size 9 (5.5mm) needles and A, cast on 30 sts.
Starting with a K row, work in St st for 36 rows, ending with RS facing for next row. Bind off.

Finishing

EMBELLISHMENT

Using photograph as a guide, thread short pieces of unspun silk or linen fibers through all the knitted pieces in a random pattern. Use a crochet hook to "hook" strands through the knitting and ensure that each "stitch" is at least 2 knitted sts long (see Special Note).

Following instructions on pages 28–29, make six evenly spaced vertical pleats, each about 1¼" (3cm) long, across top edge of each Side of Bag starting just below contrasting ruffle section, and sew securely in place.

BAG SEAMS

Using a blunt-ended yarn needle, sew Sides together along row-end and bound-off edges.

FELTING

Machine wash completed Bag and Pocket at 140°F (60°C) on a full cycle with maximum spin, using laundry detergent but no fabric conditioner.

Once pieces have been washed, remove any stray fluff and gently ease them into their correct shapes. Leave to dry naturally with right side up.

Once dry, remove threads holding pleats in place.

INNER RUFFLE

With WS facing and cast-on edge of Side toward you and using size 6 (4mm) needles and C, carefully pick up and knit 58 sts evenly across color-change row at base of ruffle.

Row 1 Knit.

Row 2 Purl.

Row 3 *K1, inc in next st; rep from * to end. *87 sts.*

Row 4 Purl.

Row 5 K1, *inc in next st, K1; rep from * to end. *130 sts.*

Row 6 Purl.

Row 7 Rep row 3. *195 sts.*

Row 8 Purl.

Bind off very loosely.

Work Inner Ruffle across other Side of Bag in same way.

Using a blunt-ended yarn needle, sew together row-end edges of Inner Ruffles. Cover Inner Ruffle pick-up row with ribbon and slip-stitch neatly in place.

ASSEMBLY

Using a sharp-pointed needle on all felted pieces, sew Pocket (with bound-off edge at top) to inside of one Side of Bag.

Sew handles inside upper edge of Bag. Sew on snap to close top of Bag.

woven-in strands

Using this technique on felted knitting is a great way to exercise your creativity. Various strands—such as lengths of unspun silk or linen fibers, ribbons, fancy yarns, and so on— are threaded through the knitting before it is felted. Once the knitting is felted, the woven-in strips, which will resist felting, are trapped in the fabric. The fibers, while resistant to the felting, are stressed by the heat and agitation and take on a new and pleasing appearance as well.

You can also weave in materials that will felt, such as wool yarns or unspun pieces of fleece (these are tops with which hand-felters work). These fibers will felt along with your knitting and can look clumpy, so if you want to experiment, as always, do a test swatch and try it out on that first (see page 106 for how to make test swatches).

One of the attractive features of this technique is that it is not uniform, so any ends of the fibers that you leave on the right side of the work will be a little shaggy after felting. If they are too untidy, you can give them a hair cut once the felted piece is dry.

After the felting process, the woven-in threads are trapped into the felted fabric and the firmness of the anchor will depend on the density of the felt. If you really try, you will be able to pull them out, leaving a small hole, so be careful not to!

Weaving in strands

With the right side of the knitting facing and using a crochet hook, pull the length of unspun silk or linen fibers (or ribbon) through the knitting, leaving an end about ¾" (2cm) long free on the right side.

Next, hook the strip through the knitting about three or four knitted stitches away from where you started as shown (see top right). I usually work horizontally across the knitting but as long as the strand is trapped under and

over at least two knitted stitches, it will hold. Repeat this hooking process for the length required, but be sure not pull the strand too tightly through the knitting. When the weaving-in is complete, snip off the end of the strand, leaving an end about ¾" (2cm) long on the right side of the work.

Next, ease out the embroidered stitches on the right side of the work so that they are not flat on the surface— there should be a little bit of slackness on right side. For this technique, more is best because very sparse woven-in areas can look a little lost after felting.

Once the woven-in strands are complete, felt the decorated knitting according to the instructions in the knitting pattern. When the knitting has been washed, gently pull into shape and leave to dry.

Use a crochet hook to weave in strands

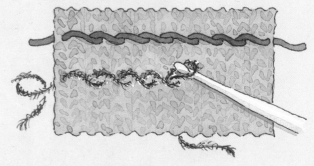

For an interesting result, use strands in contrasting textures

dots and bars blanket

Rowan's *Scottish Tweed 4-Ply* makes the softest knitted felt I have found. You know how pure wool can itch slightly? Well, felting largely takes this away, because it changes the actual structure of the wool fibers.

So this little blanket is even soft enough to become a baby blanket. Because it is made in small squares, it is a great project for knitting on the move. Half the squares have small bobbles knitted into them and half have ridges picked up across some rows, which, when felted, become uniform bars. The bobble and bars give the blanket great texture. For a larger version, just work more squares.

Finished size
Completed blanket measures approximately 25" (64cm) wide by 41½" (106cm) long.

Yarn
15 x ⅞oz (25g) balls of Rowan *Scottish Tweed 4-Ply* in **A** (Machair 002) and 4 balls in **B** (Porridge 024)

Needles
Pair of size 3 (3.25mm) knitting needles
Size 3 (3.25mm) circular knitting needle, 24" (60cm) long

Gauge before felting
26 sts and 38 rows to 4" (10cm) measured over stockinette stitch using size 3 (3.25mm) needles *or size necessary to obtain correct gauge.*

Abbreviations
MB (make bobble) = [K1, P1, K1, P1, K1] all into next st, turn, P5, turn, K5, turn, P2tog, P1, P2tog, turn, sl 1, K2tog, psso. See also page 109.

Special note
Because the bobbles are worked in a different color than the rest of the row, strand the bobble yarn loosely across the wrong side of the work from one bobble to the next, weaving it into the wrong side of the work every 3 or 4 stitches.
Ensure that the main color is taken tightly across the back of the bobble so that the bobble stands out from the knitting.
However, if your are using a light color for the background and a dark color for the bobbles, use a separate length of yarn for each bobble—otherwise the stranded bobble yarn might show through to the front once the piece is felted.

Bobble squares (make 30)
Using size 3 (3.25mm) needles and A, cast on 31 sts.
Starting with a K row, work in St st for 6 rows, ending with RS facing for next row.
Join in B.
Row 7 (RS) K3 with A, *MB with B, K1 tbl with A, K6 with A; rep from * to last 4 sts, MB with B, K3 with A.
Cut off B.
Using A, cont in St st for 13 rows, ending with RS facing for next row.
Join in B.
Row 21 (RS) K7 with A, *MB with B, K1 tbl with A, K6 with A; rep from * to end.
Cut off B.
Using A, cont in St st for 13 rows.
Join in B.
Row 35 Rep row 7.
Cut off B.
Using A, cont in St st for 7 rows.
Bind off.

Bars squares (make 30)
Using size 3 (3.25mm) needles and A, cast on 31 sts.
Starting with a K row, work in St st for 6 rows, ending with RS facing for next row.
Join in B.
Using B, cont in St st for 7 rows.
Row 14 (WS) Using B, P tog first st with corresponding st of first row worked in B, *P tog next st with corresponding st of first row in B; rep from * to end.
Cut off B.
Using A, cont in St st for 10 rows.
Rep last 18 rows once more, then first 8 of these rows again, ending with RS facing for next row.
Cut off B.
Using A, cont in St st for 8 rows. Bind off.

Finishing

SEAMS

Using a blunt-ended yarn needle and A, sew Squares together to make a rectangle six squares wide by 10 squares long. (Keep squares upright, sewing cast-on edges to bound-off edges.)

FELTING

Machine wash joined Squares at 140°F (60°C) on a full cycle with maximum spin, using laundry detergent but no fabric conditioner. Once Blanket has been washed, remove any stray fluff and gently ease it into shape. Leave to dry naturally with right side up.

SIDE BORDERS (both alike)

With RS facing, using size 3 (3.25mm) circular needle and B, pick up and knit 200 sts evenly along longer side edges of Blanket.

Row 1 (WS) Inc in first st, K to last st, inc in last st. Bind off.

END BORDERS (both alike)

With RS facing, using size 3 (3.25mm) circular needle and B, pick up and knit 128 sts evenly along shorter end edges of felted section of Blanket.

Row 1 (WS) Inc in first st, K to last st, inc in last st. Bind off.

Using a blunt-ended yarn needle, sew row-end edges of Borders together at corners.

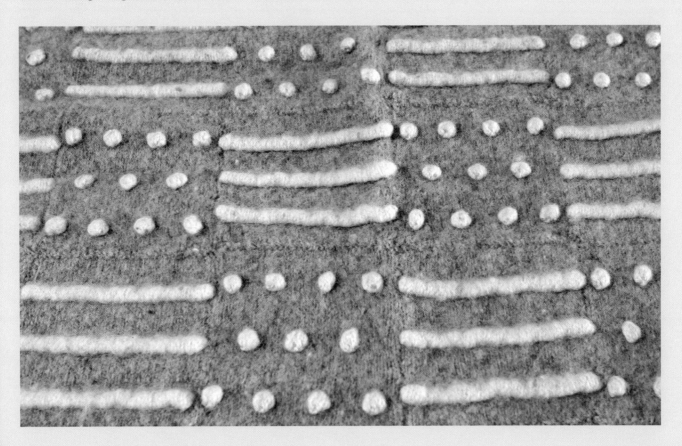

dots and bars cushion cover

Peppered with large and small knitted-in bobbles and textural felted bars, in a design similar to the blanket on page 62, this large cushion cover is just great fun to knit. Knitters will love making the bobbles and picked-up ridges. And after felting, the softened Rowan *Scottish Tweed DK* yarn is a pleasure to snuggle up to.

If you wish, you can combine this cushion with the Bobble Cushion (see page 20) or knit it in a colorway that goes well with the Dots and Bars Blanket to make a set.

Finished size

Completed cover fits a 19" (48cm) square pillow form.

Yarn

7 x 1¾oz (50g) balls of Rowan *Scottish Tweed DK* in **A** (Midnight 023) and 2 balls in **B** (Lavender 005)

Needles

Pair of size 6 (4mm) knitting needles

Notions

18" (46cm) zipper

Gauge before felting

21 sts and 29 rows to 4" (10cm) measured over stockinette stitch using size 6 (4mm) needles *or size necessary to obtain correct gauge*.

Abbreviations

MB (make bobble—first bobble version) = [K1, P1, K1, P1, K1] all into next st, turn, P5, turn, K5, turn, P2tog, P1, P2tog, turn, sl 1, K2tog, psso.
MMB (make bobble—second bobble version) = [K1, P1, K1] all into next st, turn, P3, turn, K3tog tbl.
See also page 109.

Special note

Because the bobbles are worked in a different color than the rest of the row, strand the bobble yarn loosely across the wrong side of the work from one bobble to the next, weaving it into the wrong side of the work every 3 or 4 stitches. Ensure that the main color is taken tightly across the back of the bobble so that the bobble stands out from the knitting.

However, if your are using a light color for the background and a dark color for the bobbles, use a separate length of yarn for each bobble—otherwise the stranded bobble yarn might show through to the front once the piece is felted.

Sides (make 2)

Using size 6 (4mm) needles and A, cast on 106 sts.
Starting with a K row, work in St st for 10 rows, ending with RS facing for next row.
Join in B.
Row 11 (RS) K7 with A, *MB with B, K1 tbl with A, K10 with A; rep from * to last 3 sts, K3 with A.
Cut off B.
Using A, cont in St st for 19 rows, ending with RS facing for next row.
Join in B.
Row 31 (RS) K13 with A, *MB with B, K1 tbl with A, K10 with A; rep from * to last 9 sts, MB with B, K1 tbl with A, K7 with A.
Cut off B.
Using A, cont in St st for 19 rows.
Join in B.
Row 51 Rep row 11.
Cut off B.
Using A, cont in St st for 19 rows.
Join in B.
Using B, cont in St st for 7 rows.
Row 78 (WS) Using B, P tog first st with corresponding st of first row worked in B, *P tog next st with corresponding st of first row in B; rep from * to end.
Cut off B.
Using A, cont in St st for 10 rows.
Rep last 18 rows twice more, ending with RS facing for next row.
Join in B.
Row 125 (RS) K5 with A, *MMB with B, K1 tbl with A, K6 with A; rep from * to last 5 sts, MMB with B, K1 tbl with A, K3 with A.
Cut off B.
Using A, cont in St st for 11 rows.

If you are adapting this pattern to make a cover of a different size, make sure the test swatches are completely dry before measuring the post-felting gauge. (See page 106 for how to make test swatches.)

Last 12 rows form patt for remainder of Side.
Cont in patt until Side measures 30½" (78cm), ending with RS facing for next row. (**Note:** So that bobbles are not too close to the edge, ensure that you have at least 5 rows in A after the last bobble row.)
Bind off.

Finishing

FELTING

Machine wash the Sides at 140°F (60°C) on a full cycle with maximum spin, using laundry detergent but no fabric conditioner. Once Sides have been washed, remove any stray fluff and gently ease them into shape. Leave to dry naturally with right side up.

SEAMS

Matching pattern, sew together Sides along three edges using a sharp-pointed needle. Sew zipper into an opening along fourth edge.

flower bag

Sturdy, yet very pretty, this medium-size bag has small rigid handles and an inner pocket. Inspired by felted and embroidered fabric, it is embroidered with random swirls on one side prior to felting (see page 75). Large felted flowers are added to the other side to give a dramatic impact.

The fabric that results from felting the knitted Rowan *Kid Classic* yarn is soft but very durable and strong, so the bag does not need lining.

Choose one of the two colorways for the bag, or make them both to go with different outfits—you can never have too many bags!

Finished size

Completed bag measures approximately 11¾" (30cm) wide, 9½" (24cm) tall, and 2¼" (6cm) deep.

Yarn

2 x 1¾oz (50g) balls of Rowan *Kid Classic* in **A** (Cherry Red 847 or Glacier 822) and 4 balls in **B** (Smoke 831 or Nightly 846)

Needles

Pair of size 8 (5mm) knitting needles

Notions

Optional beads—approximately 70 4mm glass beads in each of 2 colors to match each color of yarn, for flower centers
Pair of U-shaped bag handles, 5½" (14cm) wide

Gauge before felting

19 sts and 25 rows to 4" (10cm) measured over stockinette stitch using size 8 (5mm) needles *or size necessary to obtain correct gauge*.

Abbreviations

See page 109.

Sides (make 2)

Using size 8 (5mm) needles and A, cast on 70 sts.
Starting with a K row, work in St st for 15 rows, ending with WS facing for next row.
Row 16 (WS) Knit (to form fold line).
Starting with a K row, work in St st for 14 rows, ending with RS facing for next row.
Cut off A and join in B.
Row 31 (RS) K2, M1, K to last 2 sts, M1, K2.
Mark each end of last row with a cotton thread.

Cont in St st throughout and working all increases as set by last row, inc 1 st at each end of 4th row and every foll 4th row to 78 sts, then on every foll 8th row until there are 84 sts.
Work even until Side measures 18½" (47cm) from cast-on edge, ending with RS facing for next row.
Bind off.

Gusset

Using size 8 (5mm) needles and A, cast on 16 sts.
Starting with a K row, work in St st until Gusset, unstretched and starting and ending at markers, fits down one row-end edge to bound-off edge, across bound-off edge, and then up other row-end edge, ending with RS facing for next row.
Bind off.

Pocket

Using size 8 (5mm) needles and B, cast on 14 sts.
Row 1 (RS) K1, inc in next st, K to last 3 sts, inc in next st, K2.
Row 2 P2, M1, P to last 2 sts, M1, P2.
Row 3 K2, M1, K to last 2 sts, M1, K2. *20 sts.*
Cont in St st throughout and working all increases as set by last 2 rows, inc 1 st at each end of next 10 rows, then on foll 2 alt rows. *44 sts.*
Work even until Pocket measures 6¼" (16cm), ending with RS facing for next row.
Next row (RS) K1, K2tog tbl, K to last 3 sts, K2tog, K1.
Working all decreases as set by last row, dec 1 st at each end of 2nd row and foll 2 alt rows. *36 sts.*
Work 1 row, ending with RS facing for next row.
Cut off yarn B and join in yarn A. Bind off.

Large flower petals (make 4)

Using size 8 (5mm) needles and A, cast on 7 sts.
Row 1 (RS) K1, [inc in next st, K2] twice. *9 sts.*
Row 2 P2, M1, P to last 2 sts, M1, P2.
Row 3 K2, M1, K to last 2 sts, M1, K2. *13 sts.*

Cont in St st throughout and working all increases as set by last 2 rows, inc 1 st at each end of next 4 rows, then on foll 2 alt rows. *25 sts.*

Work 5 rows, ending with RS facing for next row.

Row 17 (RS) K1, K2tog tbl, K to last 3 sts, K2tog, K1. *23 sts.*

Row 18 Purl.

Row 19 K1, K2tog tbl, K to last 3 sts, K2tog, K1.

Row 20 P1, P2tog, P to last 3 sts, P2tog tbl, P1.

Rep last 2 rows 3 times more, then row 19 again, ending with WS facing for next row. *5 sts.*

Row 28 (WS) P1, [P2tog] twice. *3 sts.*

Row 29 K3tog and fasten off.

Small flower petals (make 4)

Using size 8 (5mm) needles and B, cast on 5 sts.

Row 1 (RS) K1, [inc in next st, K2] twice. *7 sts.*

Row 2 P2, M1, P to last 2 sts, M1, P2.

Row 3 K2, M1, K to last 2 sts, M1, K2. *11 sts.*

Cont in St st throughout and working all increases as set by last 2 rows, inc 1 st at each end of next 4 rows, then on foll alt row. *21 sts.*

Work 4 rows, ending with WS facing for next row.

Row 14 (WS) P1, P2tog, P to last 3 sts, P2tog tbl, P1. *19 sts.*

Row 15 Knit.

Row 16 P1, P2tog, P to last 3 sts, P2tog tbl, P1.

Row 17 K1, K2tog tbl, K to last 3 sts, K2tog, K1.

Rep last 2 rows twice more, then row 16 again, ending with RS facing for next row. *5 sts.*

Row 23 (RS) K1, K2tog tbl, K2tog. *3 sts.*

Row 24 P3tog and fasten off.

Large flower center

Using size 8 (5mm) needles and A, cast on 88 sts.

Row 1 (RS) [K2tog] 44 times. *44 sts.*

Rows 2 and 3 Knit.

Row 4 [K2tog] 22 times. *22 sts.*

Row 5 Knit.

Row 6 [K2tog] 11 times.

Cut off yarn and thread through rem 11 sts. Pull up tight and sew in yarn end securely.

Small flower center

Using size 8 (5mm) needles and B, cast on 60 sts.

Row 1 (RS) [K2tog] 30 times. *30 sts.*

Row 2 Knit.

Row 3 [K2tog] 15 times.

Cut off yarn and thread through rem 15 sts. Pull up tight and sew in yarn end securely.

Finishing

EMBELLISHMENT (OPTIONAL)

Using a blunt-ended yarn needle and a contrasting color (B or A), embroider random swirls in chain stitch on one Side of Bag and on Pocket as shown (see opposite page). With felting, the embroidery needs to be big and bold. Subtle and small shapes can get lost in the process and end up looking like clumps of color, so keep the design bold and don't embroider the lines too close together.

FLOWERS

Lay each set of Flower Petals flat with their fasten-off points meeting at center. Using a blunt-ended yarn needle, sew together Petals for about ¾" (2cm) from fasten-off point.

BAG SEAMS

Using a blunt-ended yarn needle and matching cast-on and bound-off edges of Gusset to first row of Sides in B (at markers), sew Gusset to Sides along row-end and bound-off edges. Fold first 15 rows of Sides to inside along fold-line row and sew in place.

FELTING

Machine wash the Bag, Pocket, Flowers, and Flower Centers at 104°F (40°C) on a short wash cycle (economy or quick wash options) with maximum spin for that cycle, using laundry detergent but no fabric conditioner; add an old towel to the machine to ensure adequate agitation. Once pieces have been washed, remove any stray fluff and gently ease them into their correct shapes. Leave to dry naturally with right sides up.

ASSEMBLY

Using a sharp-pointed needle, sew Pocket (with bound-off edge at top) to inside of one Side of Bag, sew on bag handles, sew Flowers to Side of Bag, and sew Flower Centers to center of Flowers, using photograph as a guide.

BEAD STAMENS (OPTIONAL)

Make two strings of beads, threading them onto toning color yarn, for each flower center—one of 40 beads and one of 30 beads. Form into loops and sew to center of Flowers.

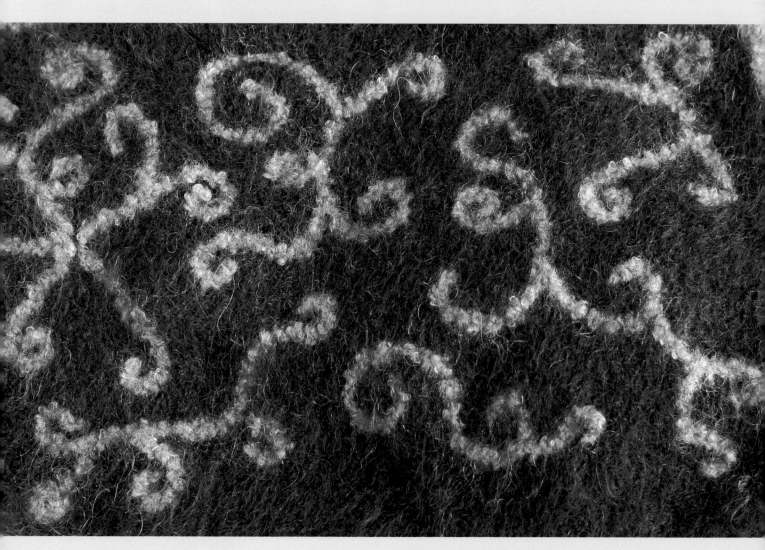

striped scarf

Making this beautifully soft and cozy felted scarf would be a great introduction to the art of knitted felt.

Knitted in two subtly contrasting colors of Rowan *Scottish Tweed 4-Ply* yarn, the scarf stripes are worked vertically using the simple intarsia technique. Before being felted, the knitting is tightly hand-pleated along the stripes with shrink-resistant thread. This pleating resists the felting process, leaving fascinating and subtle texture and color combinations once the holding stitches are removed.

I designed the scarf in two colorways so you can take your pick. But don't hesitate to try out your own color schemes.

Finished size

Completed scarf measures approximately 8¾" (22cm) wide by 44¾" (114cm) long.

Yarn

6 x ⅞oz (25g) balls of Rowan *Scottish Tweed 4-Ply* in **A** (Mallard 020 or Oatmeal 025) and 3 balls in **B** (Sea Green 006 or Thatch 018)

Needles

Pair of size 3 (3.25mm) knitting needles

Notions

Shrink-resistant thread (such as Anchor six-strand cotton embroidery floss), for sewing pleats in place

Gauge before felting

26 sts and 38 rows to 4" (10cm) measured over stockinette stitch using size 3 (3.25mm) needles *or size necessary to obtain correct gauge.*

Abbreviations

See page 109.

Scarf

Using size 3 (3.25mm) needles and A, cast on 89 sts.
Using a separate ball (or bobbin) of yarn for each vertical stripe and twisting yarns together on WS where they meet to avoid holes forming, work in patt as follows:
Row 1 (RS) K13 with A, [K6 with B, K13 with A] 4 times.
Row 2 P13 with A, [P6 with B, P13 with A] 4 times.
These 2 rows form vertical stripe patt.
Work in vertical stripe patt until almost all yarn has been used up.
Using A, bind off all sts.

Finishing

EMBELLISHMENT

Using photograph as a guide and following instructions on pages 28–29, fold each stripe in B in half lengthwise with wrong sides together and sew securely along length of scarf to form a long pleat. When sewing pleats in place, use shrink-resistant thread and a blunt-ended yarn needle, and stitch through two layers of knitting, placing stitches approximately 1¼" (3cm) apart all along pleat.

FELTING

Machine wash completed Scarf at 140°F (60°C) on a full cycle with maximum spin, using laundry detergent but no fabric conditioner.
Once Scarf has been washed, remove any stray fluff and gently ease it into shape. Leave to dry naturally with right side up.
Once Scarf is dry, remove threads securing pleats so that pleats spring into place.

hearts throw

This throw is knitted in large squares of Rowan *Scottish Tweed DK*, which makes a lovely soft felt. It is also very versatile: thick enough to double up as a rug and soft enough to be used as a toddler's blanket.

It's very easy knitting. All the effort is in the heart shapes, which are embroidered on in wool before the felting and in cotton after the felting. The appliqué heart motifs are cut from felted squares of Rowan *Kid Classic* and embroidered before they are sewn to the throw. If you prefer, you can work the throw edging in blanket stitch instead of crochet.

Finished size

Completed throw measures 32¼" (82cm) wide by 43¼" (110cm) long.

Yarn

6 x 1¾oz (50g) balls of Rowan *Scottish Tweed DK* in each of **A** (Purple Heather 030) and **B** (Lavender 005)
3 x 1¾oz (50g) balls of Rowan *Kid Classic* in **C** (Royal 835)

Needles

Pair of size 6 (4mm) knitting needles
Pair of size 8 (5mm) knitting needles
Size G-6 (4mm) crochet hook

Notions

Anchor six-strand cotton embroidery floss—approximately 3 skeins in each of 2 colors that gently tone in with yarn colors

Gauge before felting

21 sts and 28 rows to 4" (10cm) measured over stockinette stitch using A and size 6 (4mm) needles *or size necessary to obtain correct gauge.*

Abbreviations

See page 109.

Special note

When working the crochet edging around the throw, you may find it tricky to get the hook through the felted fabric. If you do, use a meat skewer to make regular holes through the fabric along the edge in the positions where the hook must pierce the fabric. These holes won't show on the finished work, but will make it much easier to crochet the edging. If you can't crochet, edge the throw with of blanket stitch instead, using a sharp-pointed needle.

Squares (make 12)

Using size 6 (4mm) needles and A, cast on 66 sts.
Starting with a K row, work in St st for 108 rows, ending with RS facing for next row.
Bind off.
Using A, make five more squares in same way.
Using B, make six more squares in same way.

Knitted appliqué fabric

Using size 8 (5mm) needles and C, cast on 100 sts.
Starting with a K row, work in St st until almost all of yarn C has been used up, setting some aside for sewing appliqué heart motifs to throw, allowing enough to bind off, and ending with RS facing for next row.
Bind off.

Finishing

EMBELLISHMENT

Using a blunt-ended yarn needle and B, embroider heart shapes in chain stitch on the Squares in A. Use the photograph on page 80 as a guide for the embroidery, placing two, three, or four hearts on each Square. Work them at random—not neatly placed, but scattered around. The hearts need to be bold and well shaped because any small, delicate or vaguely shaped hearts will be lost in the felting process and end up looking like eggs!

THROW

Using a blunt-ended yarn needle, sew all 12 Squares together in a checkerboard design to make one large rectangle three squares wide and four squares long.

FELTING

Machine wash joined Squares and Knitted Appliqué Fabric in separate washes. Machine wash joined Squares at 140°F (60°C) and Knitted Appliqué Fabric at 104°F (40°C), both on a full cycle with maximum spin and using laundry detergent but no fabric conditioner.

Once the pieces have been washed, remove any stray fluff and gently ease them into shape. Leave to dry naturally with right side up.

APPLIQUÉ AND EMBROIDERY

Make a heart-shaped template about 3½" (9cm) wide by 5" (12.5cm) tall, or use largest heart template on page 110. Using template, cut out six hearts from the felted Appliqué Fabric. (The felted pieces will not unravel when cut, so there is no need to finish the cut edges in any way.)

Using a sharp-pointed needle and all six strands of cotton embroidery floss, embroider words (such as "sleep," "hush," "zzz," and "ssh") on four of the hearts in chain stitch, and sprinkle a few lazy daisy flowers over some of the hearts. On the joined Squares, outline the felted embroidered hearts with lines of chain stitch in six-strand cotton embroidery floss, adding a curl and swirl here and there.

Using a sharp-pointed needle and lengths of C set to one side, sew the appliqué hearts to the Squares in B with chain stitches or simple running stitch. Offset placement of these hearts so that they echo scattered embroidered and felted hearts on other Squares.

EDGING

Note: See Special Note before beginning edging.

With RS facing and using size G-6 (4mm) crochet hook, work crochet edging around entire outer edge of throw, positioning single crochet stitches ³⁄₈" (1cm) apart and same distance from edge, as follows:

Join A with a slip stitch to outer edge of joined Squares, chain 1, 1 single crochet into same place as slip stitch, *1 single crochet into edge, chain 1; rep from * to end, join with a slip stitch to first single crochet and fasten off.

twist scarf

This twirled scarf is highly decorative, with beads down the outside edge highlighting the spiral shape. Simple short-row shaping contorts the knitted fabric, and the felting then emphasizes the shaping, nicely tightening up the whole thing.

There is a choice of two shades, but if you don't like either of these, take your pick from the Rowan *Scottish Tweed 4-Ply* palette.

Finished size

Completed scarf measures approximately 4" (10cm) wide by 53" (135cm) long.

Yarn

8 x 7/8oz (25g) balls of Rowan *Scottish Tweed 4-Ply* (Storm Grey 004 or Rose 026)

Needles

Pair of size 5 (3.75mm) knitting needles

Notions

Approximately 460 crystal or white 4mm glass beads

Gauge before felting

21 sts and 29 rows to 4" (10cm) measured over stockinette stitch using yarn DOUBLE and size 5 (3.75mm) needles *or size necessary to obtain correct gauge.*

Abbreviations

bead 1 = bring yarn to front (RS) of work between two needles, slide bead up next to st just worked, slip next stitch purlwise from left needle to right needle and take yarn back (WS) of work between two needles leaving bead sitting on RS of work in front of slipped st.

wrap next st = on a knit row, slip next st from left needle onto right needle, take yarn to front of work between two needles, then slip same st back onto left needle.

See also page 109.

Special note

The scarf is worked with two strands of yarn held together, but the beads should be threaded onto only one of the strands. Thread approximately 115 beads onto each of four balls. See page 17 for bead-threading tips.

Scarf

Thread beads onto yarn (see Special Note).

Using size 5 (3.75mm) needles and two strands of yarn held together (one with the beads and one without), cast on 22 sts.

Row 1 K11, P11.

Now work beaded spiral patt as follows:

Patt row 1 K1, bead 1, K7, wrap next st and turn.

(**Note:** On the rows following the rows the beads have been placed on, purl the stitches behind the beads firmly to encourage the beads to remain at the front of the work.)

Patt row 2 P9.

Patt row 3 K7, wrap next st and turn.

Patt row 4 P7.

Patt row 5 K5, wrap next st and turn.

Patt row 6 P5.

Patt row 7 K5, [K wrapped st and wrapping loop lying horizontally across front of it together as one st, K1] 3 times, P11.

These 7 patt rows form beaded spiral patt.

Work in beaded spiral patt until all yarn has been used up, leaving enough to bind off.

Bind off.

Finishing

FELTING

Machine wash completed Scarf at 140°F (60°C) on a full cycle with maximum spin, using laundry detergent but no fabric conditioner.

Once Scarf has been washed, remove any stray fluff and gently ease it into shape. Leave to dry naturally with right side up.

nursery motif hangings

Very easy, very pretty, and great for using up leftover yarns, these little motifs make a perfect project for the first-time felter. Hang them on a door or cupboard handle, or from a mantelpiece. Make as many as you wish, and mix the motifs—hearts, moons, and stars—if you like.

The decorations are cut out of rectangles of felted Rowan *Kid Classic*. Once felted the knitting will not unravel when cut into motif shapes. Two balls of each shade will easily make four to six decorations.

You can get a similar felt by using Rowan *Felted Tweed*, but if you choose this yarn, be sure to wash it at the higher temperature (see the Yarn Felting Table on page 105).

Finished size

Completed hearts measure approximately 3½" (9cm) wide by 5" (12.5cm) tall.

Completed star measures approximately 3½" (9cm) in diameter.

Completed moon crescents measure approximately 2¾" (7cm) wide by 3" (8cm) tall.

Yarn

2 x 1¾oz (50g) balls of Rowan *Kid Classic* in each of **A** (Lavender Ice 841) and **B** (Royal 835)

Note: This is sufficient yarn to make 4–6 decorations.

Needles

Pair of size 8 (5mm) knitting needles

Notions

2 crystal 4mm glass beads for string of hearts

Approximately 27½" (70cm) of ¼" (6mm) wide ribbon for each string of motifs

Gauge before felting

19 sts and 25 rows to 4" (10cm) measured over stockinette stitch using size 8 (5mm) needles *or size necessary to obtain correct gauge.*

Abbreviations

See page 109.

Knitted motif fabrics (make 2)

Using size 8 (5mm) needles and A, cast on 80 sts.

Starting with a K row, work in St st until almost all yarn A has been used up, leaving enough to bind off.

Bind off.

Make a second piece in same way, but using B.

Finishing

FELTING

Machine wash the knitted pieces at 104°F (40°C) on a full cycle with maximum spin, using laundry detergent but no fabric conditioner.

Once pieces have been washed, remove any stray fluff and gently ease them into shape. Leave to dry naturally with right side up.

STRING OF HEARTS

Make your own heart-shaped template 3½" (9cm) wide by 15" (12.5cm) tall, or use template on page 110. Cut out two more heart templates—one smaller than the first, and a third tiny one—again making your own or using templates provided.

Using heart templates, cut out two large and two tiny hearts from one piece of felted fabric. From other piece of felted fabric, cut out one large, two medium-size, and one tiny heart. (The felted pieces will not unravel when cut, so there is no need to finish the cut edges in any way.)

Make a 5½–6" (14–15cm) loop at one end of length of ribbon and sew in place.

Lay one tiny heart on one medium-size heart, then these two hearts on one large heart, alternating colors of hearts. Using a sharp-pointed needle, sew all pieces together at center by stitching on a bead through all layers.

Make another group of layered hearts in same way.

Sew first layered group of hearts to ribbon at base of loop, and remaining tiny heart to free end of ribbon, 3" (8cm) from end. Sew on remaining two large hearts (one layered, one plain) evenly spaced between hearts already in place.

STRING OF MOON CRESCENTS AND STARS

Make a star-shaped template about 3½" (9cm) in diameter, and a crescent moon-shaped template, about 2¾" (7cm) wide by 3" (8cm) tall, or use the templates on page 110. Using templates, cut out two moons from one piece of felted fabric. Cut out one star from other piece of felted fabric.

(The felted pieces will not unravel when cut, so there is no need to finish the cut edges in any way.)

Make a 5½–6" (14–15cm) loop at one end of length of ribbon and sew in place.

Using a sharp-pointed needle, sew one moon to ribbon at base of loop, and remaining moon to free end of ribbon, approximately 3" (8cm) from end. Sew on star in center between moons already sewn in place.

spiral cushion cover

Make one of the two variations of this cushion cover, and if you like the result, knit the other for a pair. It is made in Rowan *Felted Tweed*, which felts into a stable and firm fabric when washed at a high temperature. This gives these highly decorated cushions a warm, thick base, perfect for showing off the designs, which are embroidered and beaded after knitting.

This is a chance to let your creativity out. The felt is like a canvas for you to work on, freestyle, using yarn, beads, and cotton embroidery floss. All four elements— the knitted felt, the felted wool embroidery, the felted-in beads, and the shiny cotton embroidery—work beautifully together.

Finished size
Completed cover fits a 17" (43cm) square pillow form.

Yarn
8 x 1¾oz (50g) balls of Rowan *Felted Tweed* in **A** (Caramel 157 or Watery 152) and small amount in **B** (Watery 152 or Caramel 157)

Needles
Pair of size 5 (3.75mm) knitting needles

Notions
4 skeins of Anchor six-strand cotton embroidery floss in a shade similar to yarn B (851 deep teal or 378 mid toffee)
Approximately 160 topaz or sea green 4mm matte glass beads
16" (41cm) zipper

Gauge before felting
23 sts and 31 rows to 4" (10cm) measured over stockinette stitch using size 5 (3.75mm) needles *or size necessary to obtain correct gauge.*

Abbreviations
See page 109.

Sides (make 2)
Using size 5 (3.75mm) needles and A, cast on 128 sts.
Starting with a K row, work in St st for 232 rows, ending with RS facing for next row.
Bind off.

Finishing
EMBELLISHMENT
Using a blunt-ended yarn needle and B, embroider random chain-stitch swirls and circles on Sides as shown. Make sure this embroidery is big and bold, leaving at least 3 knitted stitches or rows between lines because the work will shrink a lot; if insufficient space is left the gaps will close up, leaving just "blobs" of yarn.
Using A, sew beads onto knitted pieces, echoing the embroidered shapes.
FELTING
Machine wash completed Sides at 140°F (60°C) on a full cycle with maximum spin, using laundry detergent but no fabric conditioner.
Once the Sides have been washed, remove any stray fluff and ensure that all beads are sitting on the right side of the work, gently easing any that may have moved back through the knitting. Gently ease Sides into shape—be firm as the felted fabric will be very stiff. Leave to dry naturally with right side up.
FINAL EMBROIDERY
Using a sharp-pointed needle and all six strands of cotton embroidery floss, embroider random chain-stitch swirls in and around the felted and beaded designs as shown.
SEAMS
Using a sharp-pointed needle, sew together Sides along all three edges. Sew zipper into an opening along fourth edge.

hot water bottle cover

The size of this cover fits all sizes of hot water bottles, with the bottle sliding easily inside. The felted "bumps" soften in the felting process, but if you don't want "bumps" and beads on your cover, then omit them—the finished size won't be affected.

This design is also embellished with a very opulent ruffle and a pretty three-colored braided tie.

If you want to make the cover a little smaller or wish to adapt it for a small bag, take out a few rows or make fewer stripes.

Finished size

Completed cover measures approximately 11" (28cm) wide by 14½" (37cm) long, excluding ruffle.

Yarn

1 x 1¾oz (50g) ball of Rowan *Scottish Tweed DK* in **A** (Grey Mist 001), 3 balls in **B** (Purple Heather 030), and 2 balls in **C** (Lobster 017)

Needles

Pair of size 6 (4mm) knitting needles
Size 6 (4mm) circular knitting needle

Notions

Approximately 70 pink 4mm glass beads
18 marbles 15mm in diameter, for creating "bumps"
Shrink-resistant thread (such as Anchor six-strand cotton embroidery floss), for tying marbles in place

Gauge before felting

21 sts and 29 rows to 4" (10cm) measured over stockinette stitch using size 6 (4mm) needles *or size necessary to obtain correct gauge.*

Abbreviations

See page 109.

Special note

Washed at the temperature recommended in the following instructions, *Scottish Tweed DK* will shed color, so consider putting a sheet of Color Catcher™ in the washing machine when felting the knitting.

Sides (make 2)

Using size 6 (4mm) circular needle and A, cast on 300 sts.
Row 1 (RS) Knit.

Cut off A and join in B.
Row 2 Purl.
Row 3 *Sl 1, K1, psso; rep from * to end. *150 sts.*
Rows 4 and 5 Rep rows 2 and 3. *75 sts.*
Change to size 6 (4mm) needles.
Row 6 Purl.
Row 7 *K1, sl 1, K1, psso; rep from * to end. *50 sts.*
Row 8 Purl.
Cut off B and join in A.
Row 9 Knit.
Cut off A and join in B.
Starting with a P row, work in St st for 7 rows, ending with RS facing for next row.
Row 17 (RS) K3, *yo, K2tog, K4; rep from * to last 5 sts, yo, K2tog, K3.
Cont in St st throughout, work 7 rows.
Cut off B and join in A.
Work 1 row.
Cut off A and join in C.
Inc 1 st at each end of 2nd row and foll 10 alt rows. *72 sts.*
Work 1 row.
Cut off C and join in A.
Work 1 row, inc 1 st at each end of this row. *74 sts.*
**Cut off A and join in B.
Work 23 rows.
Cut off B and join in A.
Work 1 row.
Cut off A and join in C.
Work 23 rows.
Cut off C and join in A.
Work 1 row.
Rep from ** once more.
Cut off A and join in B.
Work 1 row, ending with RS facing for next row.
Dec 1 st at each end of next row and 5 foll 3rd rows. *62 sts.*
Work 2 rows, ending with RS facing for next row. Bind off.

Finishing

TIE

Cut three lengths of each A, B, and C, each 43¼" (110cm) long. Using three lengths of same color yarn for each group, braid these nine lengths together and secure ends with a separate length of yarn, leaving a tassel about 1¼" (3cm) long at each end.

EMBELLISHMENT

Using a blunt-ended yarn needle and A, embroider flowers on stripes in B as shown. For each flower, work four lazy daisy stitches radiating out from one point. Sew on a bead at center of each flower. Make sure the flowers are fairly large, and catch them open at the sides as well as at the ends. This will ensure that they still look like flowers, rather than just splodges, once they are felted! Using photograph as a guide and following instructions on page 50, position three marbles across each stripe in C and tie in place with shrink-resistant thread.

SEAMS

Using a blunt-ended yarn needle, sew together Sides along row-end and bound-off edges, leaving cast-on edges open.

FELTING

Machine wash completed Cover and Tie at 140°F (60°C) on a full cycle with maximum spin, using laundry detergent but no fabric conditioner (see Special Note).

After washing, take pieces out of the machine and immediately remove threads holding marbles in place, then remove marbles. Next, remove any stray fluff and gently ease Cover into its correct shape. Leave to dry naturally with right side up.

INSERT TIE

Thread Tie through eyelet holes of row 17 and tie at one side.

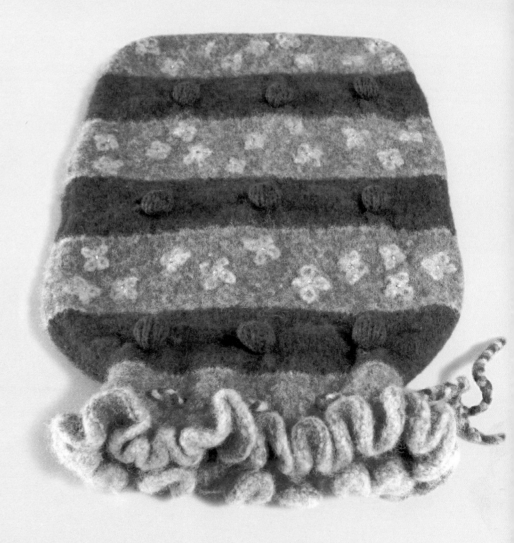

islands scarf

A piece of art-meets-clothing, this project is a little more adventurous and can be used to practice the different techniques shown in this book, because it uses several— beading, "bumps," woven-in silk, and embroidery.

The knitted island shapes in Rowan *Scottish Tweed 4-Ply* are joined together with knitted peninsulas of Rowan *Kidsilk Haze*. The wool tweed felts softly but the silk in the mohair-mix yarn resists the felting process and forms delicate ribbons instead. You could make the peninsulas shorter or longer for different effects.

Why not use whatever Shibori technique appeals most to you and make up this scarf as your own Shibori sampler?

Finished size

Completed scarf consists of a total 16 island shapes and measures approximately 74¾" (190cm) long.

Yarn

3 x ⅞oz (25g) balls of Rowan *Scottish Tweed 4-Ply* in **A** (Mallard 020) and small amount in **C** (Sea Green 006), for embroidery

1 x ⅞oz (25g) ball of Rowan *Kidsilk Haze* in **B** (Trance 582)

Needles

Pair of size 3 (3.25mm) knitting needles

Notions

Approximately 250 green-blue 3mm matte glass beads

Unspun silk fibers in a contrasting color

Approximately 22 wooden beads 10mm in diameter, for creating "bumps"

Shrink-resistant thread (such as Anchor six-strand cotton embroidery floss), for tying large wooden beads in place

Gauge before felting

26 sts and 38 rows to 4" (10cm) measured over stockinette stitch using size 3 (3.25mm) needles *or size necessary to obtain correct gauge.*

Abbreviations

bead 1 = bring yarn to front (RS) of work between two needles, slide bead up next to st just worked, slip next stitch purlwise from left needle to right needle and take yarn back (WS) of work between two needles leaving bead sitting on RS of work in front of slipped st.

(**Note:** On the rows following the rows the beads have been placed on, purl the stitches behind the beads firmly to encourage the beads to remain at the front of the work.)

See also page 109.

Scarf

FIRST (BEADED) ISLAND

Thread beads onto A (see page 17).

Using size 3 (3.25mm) needles and A, cast on 14 sts.

**Starting with a K row and following Beaded Island Chart, work in St st, placing beads as indicated on Chart *and at the same time* work shaping as follows:

Work 1 row.

Inc 1 st at each end of next 5 rows, then on foll 4 alt rows. *32 sts.*

Work 15 rows, ending with WS facing for next row.

Dec 1 st at each end of next row and foll 3 alt rows, then on foll 5 rows. *14 sts.*

Work 1 row, ending with RS facing for next row.**

This completes first island.

FIRST PENINSULA

Cut off A and join in B.

Work in St st for 12 rows, ending with RS facing for next row.

Cut off B and join in A.

This completes first peninsula.

SECOND (PLAIN) ISLAND

Work as given for first (beaded) island from ** to **, but omitting beads by replacing "bead 1" with "K1."

REMAINING PENINSULAS AND ISLANDS

Now make another peninsula exactly as before.

Cont in this way, making islands joined by peninsulas until 16 islands have been completed and working first, 3rd, 14th, and 16th islands beaded, and all other islands plain.

Once 16th island has been completed, bind off.

Finishing

EMBELLISHMENT

Using photograph as a guide and C, embroider large chain-stitch swirls on 6th, 9th, and 12th islands using a blunt-ended yarn needle. (Follow oval shape of island for swirl—once felted, it will become circular.)

Following instructions on page 50, position wooden beads

on 2nd, 5th, 11th, and 15th islands (five or six on each island) and tie in place with shrink-resistant thread.

Following instructions on pages 28–29, thread strands of silk fibers through 4th, 7th, 8th, 10th, and 13th islands.

FELTING

Machine wash the Scarf at 140°F (60°C) on a full cycle with maximum spin, using laundry detergent but no fabric conditioner.

After washing, take Scarf out of the machine and immediately remove threads holding wooden beads in place, then remove beads. Next, remove any stray fluff and ensure that all glass beads are sitting on right side of work, gently easing any that may have moved back through the knitting. Gently ease Scarf into shape. Leave to dry naturally with right side up.

BEADED ISLAND CHART

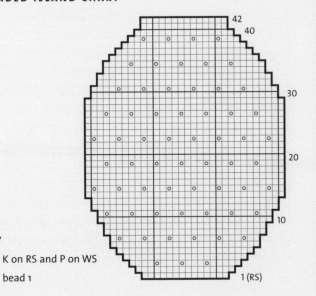

42
40

30

20

10

1 (RS)

KEY

☐ K on RS and P on WS

⊙ bead 1

felting techniques

Felting knitting is not an exact science, it's an art. Yarn shrinkage depends on a number of factors, including the type of yarn used, the yarn color, your knitting tension, and the heat of the water in the washing machine.

This may sound complicated at first, but it is much easier than you think to make felted gauge swatches and to even design your own felted knits. You do not need to master all the technical advice that follows in order to make the projects in the book, but reading it will give you an understanding of some of the felting basics and boost your confidence to make your first knitted felt. It also provides all the methods necessary for you to make simple alterations to the knits in this book and to progress to designing your own felted creations.

Suitable yarns for felting

The first question knitters new to felting will usually ask is "what yarns are suitable for felting?" As a rule, simply spun, 100 percent wool knitting yarns that have undergone few processes will felt best. Yarns that have a small nonwool content may also felt well and two of these are featured in this book. Pure wool yarns that have been treated to make them machine washable at 104°F (40°C) may not felt at all.

The longer the fibers, the more readily the yarn will felt. That is why yarns with even small amounts of mohair, which has very long fibers, must to be treated with caution when used for felted knitting.

The more processes a yarn has undergone in the dyeing, treatment, and spinning, the less well it is likely to felt. If a yarn is 100 percent wool and it feels simple and lofty, it is likely to felt better than heavily processed ones.

As a very general rule, although there are exceptions, undyed yarns (of which I have used none in this book) felt readily, while pale-colored yarns that have been treated to achieve that shade, felt slightly less readily. Dark-colored yarns felt slightly more.

I have tested all the yarns used in this book and several other Rowan yarns. The results of these tests are shown in the Yarn Felting Table (see opposite page).

Felting variables

Your knitting tension and mine will probably vary, and can affect the outcome of felting. More crucially, your washing machine and mine may create slightly different felting effects; having tested swatches in several different machines, I know this can be true. Quite small variations in temperature can affect the outcome.

For these reasons, you should take into account that the Yarn Felting Table and the resulting patterns in the book are all based on the yarn's recommended gauge and my own modern, standard front-loading washing machine, which has 140°F (60°C), 120°F (50°C), and 104°F (40°C) washing cycles. The full cycle, including the spinning, ranges from one and a half hours for the hottest wash to one hour for the 104°F (40°C) wash. My machine also has options for shorter washes for all programs and a "delicates" 104°F (40°C) cycle, which is 30 to 45 minutes long. Most machines have these standard features.

I strongly urge you to do some test-swatching if you are concerned about either your personal knitting tension or the washing machine you are using. (See page 106 for how to make test swatches.)

Yarn Felting Table

This table show how much various Rowan yarns will shrink when felted.
Gauge: All gauges given are based on the gauge recommended on the yarn label.
W = width   **L** = Length   **N/A** = not applicable
Felting washes: The felting washes are all on a full cycle (except where a short cycle is specified) with maximum spin for that cycle.

Rowan yarn	Prefelted measurement of test swatch and recommended gauge	Post-felted measurement of test swatch		
		Felted once at 104°F (40°C)	**Felted once at 140°F (60°C)**	**Felted twice at 140°F (60°C)**
Scottish Tweed 4-Ply	8" (20cm) square Gauge: 27 sts and 39 rows = 4" (10cm) square using size 3 (3.25mm) needles	N/A	W = 6⅞" (17.5cm) L = 5⅛" (13cm)	N/A
Scottish Tweed DK	8" (20cm) square Gauge: 22 sts and 30 rows = 4" (10cm) using size 6 (4mm) needles	N/A	W = 7" (18cm) L = 6" (15cm)	W = 6½" (16.5cm) L = 5⅛" (13cm)
Scottish Tweed Aran	8" (20cm) square Gauge: 16 sts and 23 rows = 4" (10cm) using size 8 (5mm) needles	N/A	W = 6¼" (16cm) L = 5½" (14cm)	W = 6" (15cm) L = 4¾" (12cm)
Scottish Tweed Chunky	8" (20cm) square Gauge: 12 sts and 16 rows = 4" (10cm) using size 11 (8mm) needles	N/A	N/A	W = 6½" (16.5cm) L = 5⅛" (13cm)
Kid Classic	8" (20cm) square Gauge: 19 sts and 25 rows = 4" (10cm) using size 8 (5mm) needles	W = 6¼" (16cm)* L = 6" (15cm)*	N/A	N/A
Country	8" (20cm) square Gauge: 10 sts and 14 rows = 4" (10cm) using size 13 (9mm) needles	W = 6½" (16.5cm)* L = 6" (15cm)*	W = 5" (12.5cm)** L = 5" (12.5cm)**	N/A
Tapestry	8" (20cm) square Gauge: 22 sts and 30 rows = 4" (10cm) using size 6 (4mm) needles	W = 4¾" (12cm) L = 4⅛" (10.5cm)	N/A	N/A
Felted Tweed	8" (20cm) square Gauge: 24 sts and 32 rows = 4" (10cm) using size 5 (3.75mm) needles	W = 7" 18cm)* L = 6" (15cm)*	W = 6" (15cm) L = 4¼" (11cm)	N/A

*This is with a short 104°F (40°C) wash cycle (30–45 minutes long, with spinning).   ** This felt is very thick and not useful for most applications.

Yarn Felting Table and felting formula

First of all, you don't need to use the Yarn Felting Table or the felting formula I have provided if you just want to knit the patterns in the book, because I have already done all the calculations. You may, however, decide that you want to test your washing machine; or you might want to change the size of one of my designs. Finally, you may soon be following me down the felting-frenzy route, in which case, you'll need to learn how to felt yarns of your choice.

Do not be alarmed by the Yarn Felting Table or the felting formula. If I can cope with these, I promise you that you can, too. They are the key to making whatever you want to knit and felt come out the right size.

The first thing you will need to do when designing felted knits is to decide what kind of felt you want to make. Do you want a durable bag or a finer scarf or wrap? This decision will influence the yarn you choose.

Having made your choice of yarn, you then need to decide how big you want the knitting to be after it has been felted and how many stitches and rows to work to achieve this size. The Yarn Felting Table (see page 105) is a guide for the shrinkage of Rowan yarns. When using this table, however, remember that it is only a guide; shrinkage can vary between washing machines and between yarn colors. So it is always essential to knit a gauge square and then felt it, especially when making size-critical pieces of felted knitting.

Making a felted test swatch

To make a felted test swatch, I recommend working a 8" (20cm) square. Using the needle size recommended on the yarn label, cast on the recommended number of stitches for 8" (20cm) and work in stockinette stitch for the recommended number rows for 8" (20cm). The number of stitches and rows for a 4" (10cm) square is usually specified on the label, so double these figures for an 8" (20cm) square. Then bind off and sew in the yarn ends. Next, pin the swatch out flat on a cloth or ironing board and carefully measure it. If your square doesn't match the recommended gauge, change your needle size until you can achieve the correct gauge—this will help to ensure that shrinkage is in line with the percentages in the Yarn Felting Table.

Once you have achieved a gauge as close as possible to the one recommended, make a note of the width and length and the number of stitches and rows you have worked. Keep a record of the needle size used as well.

Felt the test piece in the machine at whatever temperature you think you want to use and on a full cycle with maximum spin for that cycle—for example, if it is Rowan *Scottish Tweed*, you may go straight for 140°F (60°C) (see the Tips on the opposite page for more about achieving successful felting). Record the temperature and program you used. Once the swatch is fully dry, measure it again and record the new, felted measurements. Now you are ready to design your own piece of felted knitting using the felting formula.

Calculating with the felting formula

The felting formula is applied to the pre- and post-felting measurements to calculate how many stitches and rows are required to achieve a specific felted size. Here is the felting formula:

Number of stitches required = (a ÷ b) x desired width
Number of rows required = (c ÷ d) x desired length

The numbers for a, b, c, and d are as follows:
a = the number of stitches in an 8" (20cm) wide piece of knitting, using the recommended gauge BEFORE felting
b = the width of the 8" (20cm) wide piece of knitting AFTER felting
c = the number of rows in an 8" (20cm) long piece of knitting, using the recommended gauge BEFORE felting

d = the length of the 8" (20cm) long piece of knitting AFTER felting

For example, here is how to calculate how many stitches and rows to work for a finished felted square cushion cover measuring 18¾" (48cm) by 18¾" (48cm). Begin by knitting a gauge swatch as explained (see below left). Then felt the square (see below right).

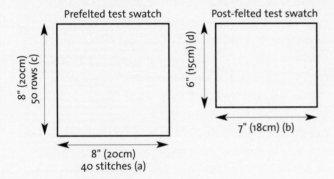

Prefelted test swatch

8" (20cm) 50 rows (c)

8" (20cm) 40 stitches (a)

Post-felted test swatch

6" (15cm) (d)

7" (18cm) (b)

Use the felting formula for inches as follows:

No. of sts required   = (40 sts ÷ 7") x 18¾"   = 107 sts
No. of rows required = (50 rows ÷ 6") x 18¾"   = 160 rows

Or, use the felting formula for centimeters as follows:

No. of sts required   = (40 sts ÷ 18cm) x 48cm   = 107 sts
No. of rows required = (50 rows ÷ 15cm) x 48cm   = 160 rows

Tips for successful felting

These are my top tips for success with your knitted felt. Be sure to follow these if you are creating your own designs or attempting to alter a project in this book.

- **Make careful test swatches:** Always knit a test square before you start a project, and make a note of the number of stitches you cast on and the rows you knitted. Measure the swatch carefully prior to felting and then again afterward—that way, you will always be able to work out the shrinkage percentages for the yarns. Keep this record for future reference; I keep a notebook with all my felting measurements in it, along with samples of the yarns, which I staple alongside the notes.

- **Remember that all yarns felt differently:** All yarns, even 100 percent wool yarns, felt in a different way and are not interchangeable.

- **Test wool yarns to see if they will felt:** Not all 100 percent wool yarns will felt. If you are considering substituting wool yarns, you must test a swatch first. If it says "machine washable" on the yarn label, the chances of it felting are low. Also, some 100 percent wool yarns actually unravel rather than felting at 140°F (60°C), due to different spinning methods used in the factory and the way that the yarn is treated to make it machine washable. Some will just stay the same. Dye treatments can influence felting as well.

- **Try the felting hand-test on the yarn:** You can hand-test a length of yarn by rolling it into a ball, adding a drop of dishwashing liquid and hand-hot water (not too hot) and rolling this about in your hands—if it seems like it's clumping up, it might well felt and it's probably worth knitting a test swatch.

- **Be aware that wool will fade when felted:** Wool isn't meant to be washed at the high temperatures used for felting. These temperatures will stress it so that it fades, often in a very attractive way.

- **Felt several test swatches together:** You can save test swatches (assuming you want to wash them at the same temperature) and felt them in one load to save time, energy, and water.

- **Use the right washing ingredients and washing cycle on test swatches:** I always use normal laundry detergent, tablets or liquid, but no fabric conditioner. Use the full cycle for the temperature being used (unless a short cycle is recommended) and the maximum spin for the chosen cycle.

- **Test each yarn color being used:** Carefully note the changes in size that different color dyes will yield.

- **Use a Color Catcher™ for knitting that has strongly contrasting colors in it:** If you are felting something that has strongly contrasting colors, add two sheets of Color Catcher™ to the wash. These sheets help absorb loose dye and prevent color from running.

- **Increase friction when felting small items:** If felting a small item, pop an old towel into the washing machine with it to increase the friction and agitation.

- **Dry test swatches thoroughly:** The felting process is not complete until the item is totally dry; if it is still damp, further slight shrinkage can take place.

- **Clean your washing machine after using it for felting:** Yarn sheds fibers when felted, so after felting wipe out the inside of the drum with a damp cloth, then run a rinse cycle on empty to avoid getting the fibers on your next wash!

- **Watch out for the effects of woven-in unspun wool:** Unspun lengths of wool tops (used for making felt by hand) will felt very readily, so experiment before weaving in strands of it over an entire project.

- **Take special care when weaving in unusual items:** Always test the fibers or items you think you can use for Shibori felting. For example, you might want to try weaving in ribbon,

fine nonprecious jewelry chains, or nonfelting fancy yarn, or tying in some unusual objects. The results can sometimes be surprising, and these test pieces won't go to waste because you can use them as the inside pockets for a bag.

- **Use shrink-resistant thread for pleating and tying:** When pleating prior to felting or when tying in an object to create "bumps," be sure to use a nonfelting, shrink-resistant thread. Rowan *4-Ply Cotton* yarn or Anchor six-strand cotton embroidery floss are ideal. If you use the wrong thread, you may not be able to get it out after felting. For example, if you tie in a marble to create a "bump" using wool yarn, the yarn tie will felt into the fabric and the marble will be trapped in the fabric.

- **Make fast pleats with clips:** If you don't want to take the time to sew pleats in place before felting, you can get a similar (but less precise) effect by holding the pleats in place with a sturdy stationery clip—but remember it has to go into your washing machine.

- **Make twisted effects with elastic bands:** Try twisting the knitting, and tying the twists in place with with rubber bands (as in tie-dyeing) before felting, but be sure to make a test swatch first.

- **Make corsages or cards from test swatches:** Use some of your test swatches afterward to cut out shapes for making corsages or cards, assuming that the felt is stable enough for the knitting not to unravel. Rowan *Kid Classic*, felted at 104°F (40°C), is best for this.

- **Use a sharp-pointed needle on felted knitting:** For hand sewing on prefelted knitting, use the usual blunt-ended yarn needle. But on post-felted knitting, you will need to use a sharp-pointed crewel embroidery needle.

Aftercare of felted knits

Even though an item has been felted, it will continue to felt if you machine wash it again on a hot program. Assuming that you don't felt it again, the Shibori features, such as the pleats and the "bumps," are permanent, so they will withstand hand washing without any problems.

A very cool machine wash might be all right for some items, such as those knitted in Rowan *Scottish Tweed*, but I always hand wash felts, then give them a brief spin, reshape, and dry flat.

Anything with Rowan *Kidsilk Haze* in it must be hand washed in accordance with instructions on the yarn label, especially if it's a ruffle detail that has been added after felting, such as on the Sheer Scarf or the Ruffled Bag.

Rigid handles on the bags in this book are all sewn on after felting, so if the bag gets grubby, you can easily unpick the stitches, hand wash the bag, and sew the handle back in again afterward.

A pleated item can be carefully scrunched together while it is drying so that the pleats close up.

Knitting abbreviations

The abbreviations below are the general ones used for the felted knitting projects in this book. Special abbreviations are given within the individual patterns.

alt	alternate
beg	begin(ning)
cm	centimeter(s)
cont	continu(e)(ing)
dec	decreas(e)(ing)
DK	double knitting (a lightweight yarn)
foll	follow(s)(ing)
g	gram(s)
in	inch(es)
inc	increas(e)(ing); increase one st by working into front and back of st
K	knit
K2tog	knit next 2 sts together
m	meter(s)
M1	make one st; pick up strand between st just knit and next st with tip of left needle, then work into back of it
mm	millimeter(s)
oz	ounce(s)
P	purl
P2tog	purl next 2 sts together
patt	pattern; or work in pattern
psso	pass slipped stitch over
rem	remain(s)(ing)
rep	repeat(s)(ing)
rev St st	reverse stockinette st; purl all sts on RS rows and knit all sts on WS rows
RS	right side
sl	slip
st(s)	stitch(es)
St st	stockinette stitch; knit all sts on RS rows and purl all sts WS rows
tbl	through back of loop(s)
tog	together
WS	wrong side
yd	yard(s)
yo	yarn over

* Repeat instructions after asterisk/s or between asterisk/s as many times as instructed.

[ ] Repeat instructions inside brackets as many times as instructed.

templates

These shapes are for the motifs on the Nursery Motif Hangings, the embroidery on the Leafy Place Mats and Coasters, and the appliqué on the Hearts Throw.
Note: All the shapes are shown at 75% of their actual size, so enlarge them by 133% before use.

STAR TEMPLATE
Use this star shape for the Nursery Motif Hangings on pages 88–91.

MOON TEMPLATE
Use this moon shape for the Nursery Motif Hangings on pages 88–91.

HEART TEMPLATES
Use these three heart shapes for the Nursery Motif Hangings on pages 88–91, and the largest heart shape for the appliqué on the Hearts Throw on pages 80–83.

LEAF TEMPLATE
Use this leaf shape for the embroidery on the prefelted Leafy Place Mats and Coasters on pages 42–45.